Shifra Stein's

A Kid's Guide to Kansas City

By

Diana Lambdin Meyer

DEDICATION

To my son Brad, who keeps me young
and makes me old simultaneously.

Diana Lambdin Meyer
A Kid's Guide to Kansas City
PO. Box 14082
Parkville, MO 64152

Cover design by Chelsey Derks

ISBN 0-9763873-0-1

Printed in the United States of America
First Printing

Table of Contents

WYANDOTTE COUNTY, KS

JOHNSON COUNTY, KS

WEEKEND GETAWAYS

Acknowledgements

As the third edition of *A Kid's Guide to Kansas City* makes its way to the public, I celebrate the tenth anniversary of my career as a fulltime freelance writer, and all of the challenges, joys and opportunities that only those who are self-employed on a fulltime basis can truly understand. In so doing, I must acknowledge Shifra Stein, my mentor and friend, who traveled this path long before others dreamed of doing so, and who accomplished so much, including the first edition of *A Kid's Guide to Kansas City*. It is truly an honor to follow in her footsteps.

It's also an honor to recognize the work of Chelsey Derks, a remarkable teenager from Olathe, who designed the cover of this edition of *A Kid's Guide to Kansas City*. This is Chelsey's rendition of the Kansas City Children's Fountain, a sculpture by Tom Corbin located in North Kansas City. Chelsey is an accomplished writer, artist, and the daughter of one of my dearest friends, so it is a true pleasure to incorporate her talents into this book. Her mother must also be recognized, for delivering design elements, for providing advice and support, and for always being there.

It's been a pleasure in working on this edition of *A Kid's Guide to Kansas City* to renew an old friendship and working relationship with Karla Martinez, a talented graphic designer who has brought a fabulous look to this book.

A new friend and great proofreader is Candy Herbert, whose skilled services are endless in a business she calls "Get It Done Personal Errand Service." She's read every word of this book and caught so many of my errors, so thanks, Candy, for your detail and professionalism.

Many, many thanks go to the hundreds of moms, businesses and enthusiastic supporters who've given great ideas and support to this effort. While the pages of the book are numbered, good ideas never can be, so continue to visit the website, **www.kckidsguide.com** for the latest happenings and information that come from so many wonderful folks throughout the Midwest. I might also mention at this point the great work of my website designer, Roger Brookbank with Swanraiser Graphics. Besides being a talented techno-geek, he's patient with me, and that's priceless.

Finally, readers of this book must know of the contributions made by my husband and son. Bruce and Brad have always encouraged me, supported me and shared in any successes I have known. They have lifted and toted heavy boxes of books, made deliveries, observations and comments that have culminated in an environment that allows me to pursue my dreams.

And thank you to you, for your interest in the lives of children in Kansas City. May *A Kid's Guide to Kansas City* make your life and theirs just a bit more enjoyable.

Notes on our Favorite Places

Introduction

Welcome to the third edition of *A Kid's Guide to Kansas City!* Just as our children grow and change before our very eyes, so does our city and this book that represents more than 700 things to do with your children. Every phone number, every address, every website and every fact has been checked so that sharing time with your children is as easy and as stress-free as possible.

Building on the format created by Shifra Stein more than 15 years ago, this edition of *A Kid's Guide to Kansas City* includes sections devoted to health and safety of our children, on family voluntarism and educational weekend getaways. You'll be impressed with the number of parks and playgrounds in our city, free for enjoyment, and the fabulous services and programs they offer.

This edition includes a new chapter on Leavenworth County, expanded history and trivia components, and an index specifically devoted to activities with teenagers. The educational activities are all but endless and only require an interested mind and the encouragement of good parents.

The purpose of this book is to remind you that time spent with children doesn't have to be costly, exotic or trivial. *A Kid's Guide to Kansas City* should reinforce to you that the City of Fountains here in the Heartland is indeed a great place to enjoy with your family. Have fun exploring together!

Finding your Way Around Kansas City

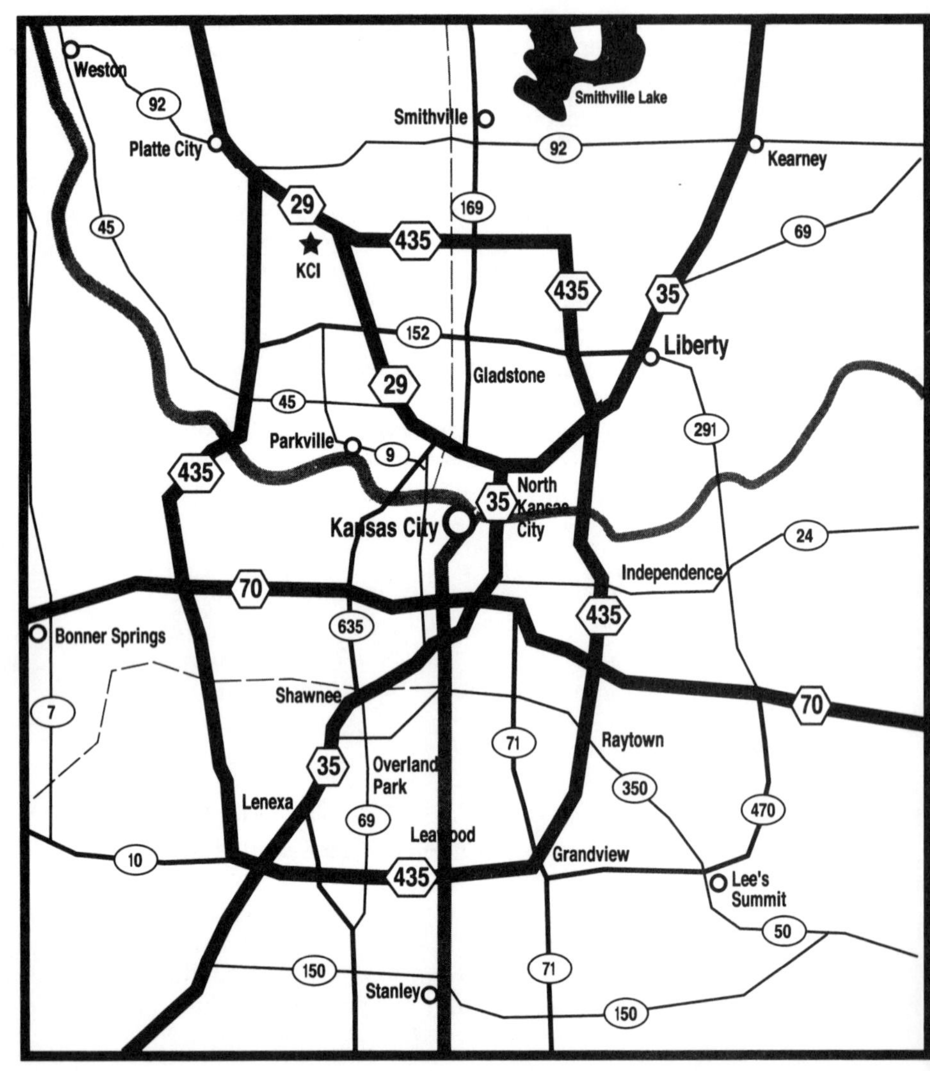

ALL AROUND THE TOWN

YOUTH DEVELOPMENT ORGANIZATIONS

Boys & Girls Clubs of Greater Kansas City, 6301 Rockhill Rd., Kansas City, MO 64131, 816-361-3600, www.bgc-gkc.org. While promoting the development of self-esteem, values and skills, programs here include reading and computer literacy, drug, alcohol and violence prevention, cultural and performing arts and recreational activities. The Clubs are home to the Reading is Fundamental (RIF) and the Reviving Baseball in the Inner City (RBI) programs. In addition, the organization provides before- and after-school child care. **Ages: 5-18.**

Unit locations are:

East Side Unit - 24th & Quincy, Kansas City, MO, 816-215-2969
Hawthorne Unit - 16995 E. Dover Lane, Independence, 816-257-7010
Leslie Unit - 432 South Leslie, Independence, 816-461-1422
John Thornberry Unit - 3831 E. 43rd St., Kansas City, MO, 816-861-6300
Troost-Midtown Unit - 3936 Troost, Kansas City, MO, 816-753-2272
Wyandotte County Unit - 1210 N. 10th St., Kansas City, KS, 913-621-3260

Before & After School Sites:

Banneker Elementary - 7050 Askew, Kansas City, MO, 816-418-1850
Melcher Elementary - 3958 Chelsea, Kansas City, MO, 816-418-6725
Milton Moore Elementary - 4510 Linwood, Kansas City, MO, 816-418-6825
Richardson Elementary - 3515 Park, Kansas City, MO, 816-418-2654
Satchel Paige Elementary - 3301 E. 75th St., Kansas City, MO, 816-418-5050
St. Monica Elementary - 5809 Michigan St., Kansas City, MO, 816-444-6736
Community Resource Lab - 1807 E. 58th St., Kansas City, MO, 816-444-0696

Camp Fire USA Heartland Council, 7930 State Line Rd., # 100, Prairie Village, KS 66208, 913-648-2121, www.kc-campfire.org/. This co-educational, diverse youth development agency serves boys and girls to build caring, confident youth and future leaders; stressing self-reliance and decision making skills in fun, informal group activity programs. Camp Shawnee, 20 minutes from Kansas City, offers resident and weekend camping programs teaching youngsters how to enjoy the beauty of nature and preserve it for the future. The Rope Challenge Course offers teambuilding exercises for youth and adults. Ask about Candy Sales. **Ages: K-12th Grade.**

Heart of America Council, Boy Scouts of America, 10210 Holmes, Kansas City, MO 64131, 816-942-9333, www.hoac-bsa.org. More than 55,000 boys in metropolitan Kansas City are members of the Boy Scouts, a national organization that since 1910 has provided an educational program to build character, to train in the responsibilities of participating citizenship, and to develop personal fitness. Boys may join at any age. Call to find a troop near you. **Ages: 6-21.**

Mid-Continent Council of Girl Scouts, 8383 Blue Parkway, Kansas City, MO 64133, 816-358-8750, www.girlscoutsmcc.org**.** More than 38,000 girls in 18 counties on both sides of the state line are Girl Scouts, with opportunities to learn a variety of life-long skills, develop a social conscience and gain a sense of belonging – all with the help and guidance of caring, committed adult volunteers. In addition to after-school troop meetings, Girl Scout programs are available during the school day, in the summer at day and resident camps, and through a wide range of specialty workshops, clinics and events offered throughout the year. **Ages: 5-17.**

YMCA of Greater Kansas City, 3100 Broadway, Kansas City, MO 64111, 816-561-9622, www.ymca-kc.org**.** For more than 150 years, the YMCA has served communities around the world. The modern Y offers child care programs, swimming and other sports lessons, and educational opportunities that focus on character development. There are 14 Y's in Kansas City, each with different services and programs to serve the needs of its community.

THE ARTS

For an updated listing of arts programs for children in Kansas City, visit www.ArtsLinks.org.

American Heartland Theatre, 2450 Grand Ave., # 314, Kansas City, MO 64108, 816-842-9999 (tickets), 816-842-0202, www.ahtkc.com**.** Located in Crown Center, this Broadway-style theatre offers fun for the entire family with special matinee and student prices. Children's acting classes are also available. **Ages: 6 and up.**

CITI'ARTS, 3800 Troost, Kansas City, MO 64109, 816-531-0949. Citi'Arts has a curriculum that consists of classes and experiences for children and teenagers in a number of areas, including piano/organ, woodwinds, brass, voice, strings, arts, ballet and drama. Scholarships, grants and mentor programs are available. Free two-week camps are offered each summer. **Ages: 5-16.**

Coterie Children's Theatre, 2450 Grand Ave., Kansas City, MO 64108, 816-474-6552, www.thecoterie.com. Named by *TIME* magazine as one of the five best theatres for young audiences in the U.S., this not-for profit professional theater is located on the lower level of Crown Center Shops. In addition to offering audiences a season of six main stage shows and a Young Playwrights' Festival, theater classes and workshops are offered year-round for ages 5-18.

The Coterie Theatre seeks to open lines of communication between races, sexes and generations by redefining children's theatre to include families and diverse audiences. **Ages: 5 and up.**

Friends of Chamber Music, 4643 Wyandotte, # 201, Kansas City, MO 64112, 816-561-9999, www.chambermusic.org. Children-oriented afternoon and family concerts are part of the Friends' programs during the school year at the Folly Theatre. Three times a year, Friends offers "What Makes It Great?", a free program for families where a particular piece of music is discussed in an age appropriate manner prior to its performance. **Ages: 7 and up.**

Folly Kids' Series, 300 W. 12th St., Kansas City, MO 64105, 816-474-4444, www.follytheater.org. This historic Kansas City theatre offers a children's series from October through April on weekday mornings, featuring visiting troupes of professionals in classic and original plays. Partnerships with renowned organizations such as The Kennedy Center at TheatreWorks USA enhance the experience for children. **Ages: 4-10.**

Kansas City Ballet, 1601 Broadway, Kansas City, MO 64108, 816-931-2232, www.kcballet.org**.** Before taking children to a performance of this award-winning ballet company, you may wish to visit the website and the children's section that includes terminology, musical notes and appropriate behavior tips, as well as games and fun facts about ballet. Then make the Kansas City tradition of a performance of "The Nutcracker" one of your family holiday traditions. A Sugar Plum Fairy luncheon is held the first Saturday of December. **Ages: 5 and up.**

Kansas City Repertory Theatre, 4949 Cherry, Kansas City, MO 64110, 816-235-2727, www.kcrep.org**.** Student matinees are presented for most of the many high-quality productions at this theatre on the University of Missouri-Kansas City campus. A Kansas City holiday tradition is taking the family to see "A Christmas Carol" at the rep. The Metropolitan Youth Company provides opportunities for talented area high school students to work with professional theatre artists **Ages: 6 and up.**

Kansas City Symphony, 1020 Central, Kansas City, MO 64105, 816-471-0400, www.kcsymphony.org**.** Who says the symphony has to be for grown-ups? This organization offers three family-oriented "sampler" concerts each year and school performances that integrate lectures on music history. Teachers are offered a curriculum guide with a CD to discuss the concert with their classes. **Ages 6-14.**

Kansas City Young Audiences, 5601 Wyandotte, Kansas City, MO 64113, 816-531-4022, www.kcya.org**.** Looking for an artistic or cultural program to bring to your school? Get a catalogue of Young Audiences performances that include music, dance, drama, creative writing, and the visual arts. The Community School of Arts offers after-school, weekend and summer classes in the same disciplines. This organization is the largest arts education provider in the Midwest, providing more than 1,000 performances and 2,000 workshops a year. **Ages: 5 and up.**

Kemper Museum of Contemporary Art, 4420 Warwick Blvd., Kansas City, MO 64111, 816-561-3737, www.kemperart.org**.** The Kemper offers more than 50 free educational programs each year, including teacher workshops and family days with hands-on activities for kids. **Ages: Preschool and up**.

Lyric Opera of Kansas City, 1029 Central, Kansas City, MO 64105, 816-471-4933, www.kc-opera.org**.** Although most productions are adult-oriented and presented in their original language, older children and teenagers might enjoy some performances. Student discounts are offered. The Opera For Kids and Opera For Teens program teaches children in elementary grades how to work together for a successful production. Singing, acting, and creating costumes and sets are all part of the fun. For younger children, the **Lyric Opera Express** visits area schools with age appropriate programs, such as *Goldilocks and the Three Bears*.

M.C. Players, 913-321-8427. This company specializes in African-American themes and actors.

Nelson-Atkins Museum of Art, 4525 Oak Street, Kansas City, MO 64111, 816-751-1278, www.nelson-atkins.org/**.** One of the nation's top general art museums, the Nelson-Atkins is full of fascinating exhibits for youngsters, including ancient Egyptian, Greek, Roman, Chinese and African works. See masterpieces by European artists such as Caravaggio, Rubens, El Greco, Cezanne and van Gogh. **Ages: preschool and up.** *(see additional information page 54)*

> **Ford Learning Center at the Nelson-Atkins Museum of Art.** The center includes seven studio classrooms where children can use direct experience with art in the galleries as a foundation for art making. **Ages: 3 and up.**
>
> **Nelson-Atkins Museum of Art School Tours, 816-561-4000.** Tours cover subjects from animals to masterpieces of European painting and history. A written request is needed two weeks in advance. **Grades 3 through 12.**

Rainbow's End Theatre, 1615 E. 18th St. Kansas City, MO 64108, 816-474-0888, www.rainbowsendtheatre.com**.** This professional theatre company offers acting programs for children, as well as performances appropriate for school groups and families throughout the year in the historic GEM Theatre in the 18th & Vine District. Rainbow's End also brings performances to your school or community group. **Ages: 5 and up.**

UMKC Conservatory of Music, 4949 Cherry, Kansas City, MO 64110, 816-235-2741, www.umkc.educ/conservatory**.** The Community Music and Dance Academy, a part of the Conservatory, provides classes for children in a wide variety of disciplines, including Suzuki piano and violin. For newborns and up, the Kindermusik program introduces the appreciation of music. Recitals for children ages three to eight, a part of the Kid's Club program, are another great way to introduce music to your children. **Ages: Newborn and up.**

Youth Symphony of Kansas City, 7301 Mission Rd, # 143, Prairie Village, KS 66208, 913-722-6810, www.youthsymphonykc.org**.** If your child is a talented musician, expand his or her opportunities through the Youth Symphony's study programs in classical symphonic, choral and chamber music. There are five orchestras, a flute choir and chamber ensembles. **Ages: 9 and up.**

SPORTS

Kansas City Chiefs, One Arrowhead Dr., Kansas City, MO 64129, 816-920-9300, www.kcchiefs.com**.** Encourage your children to practice letter writing skills by sending a letter to the Kansas City Chiefs requesting a Fan Pack. Free of charge and designed for children, this packet includes a sticker, player photos, a ruler and other Chiefs' items.

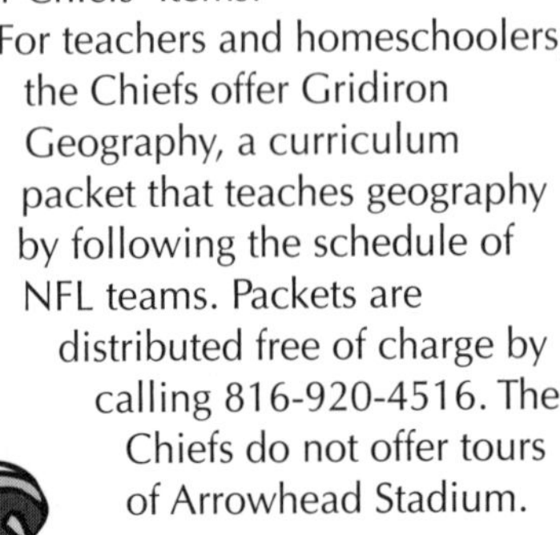

For teachers and homeschoolers, the Chiefs offer Gridiron Geography, a curriculum packet that teaches geography by following the schedule of NFL teams. Packets are distributed free of charge by calling 816-920-4516. The Chiefs do not offer tours of Arrowhead Stadium.

Kansas City Comets Professional Indoor Soccer, 1800 Genessee, # 111, Kansas City, MO 64102, 816-474-2255, www.kccomets.com**.** A Kansas City Comets game offers non-stop high-speed indoor soccer action for the whole family. Ask about the Family Four Pack and get four midfield reserve tickets, four hot dogs and four sodas for only $40. Stay in your seats at halftime for entertainment by the Galaxy Girls Dance Team and the Comets' mascot, Fuzzy the Cosmic Cat.

Youth soccer teams inquire about playing on the field before professionals play. Comets birthday parties at Kemper Arena include food and beverages and a special opportunity to meet Comets players and Fuzzy. The Comets season begins in October and ends in April. **Ages: All.**

Kansas City Explorers Tennis, P.O. Box 1521, Mission, KS 66222, 913-362-9944, www.kcexplorers.com**.** World-class tennis is played all summer at the courts on J.C. Nichols Parkway on the Country Club Plaza. It's never too early to introduce kids to the lifelong sport of tennis. **Ages: All.**

Kansas City Kite Club, www.kckiteclub.org**.** This fun group gets together to fly-kits on the second and fourth Sunday of each month at a variety of locations in the city. They also organize activities with other kite enthusiasts and travel to kite festivals together.

Kansas City Outlaws Hockey Team, 1800 Genessee, Kansas City, MO 64102, 816-513-4400, www.kansascityoutlaws.com**.** A United Hockey League Team that joined the Kansas City sports scene in 2004, the Outlaws play in Kemper Arena from October through April. In addition to the fast-paced action of three periods of play, kids will enjoy the intermission activities that often allow children on the ice for fun-filled races and competitions. Birthday packages are available. **Ages: All.**

Kansas City Royals, One Royal Way, Kansas City, MO 64129, 816-504-4040, www.kcroyals.com. Kauffman Stadium, better known as "The K," is renowned for its beautiful fountains and fireworks each time a KC Royal hits a home run. After every Friday night home game, a full fireworks display is coordinated with a lighted water display on the 12-story high fountains. Sunday is "Kids Eat Free" Day at the ballpark, when all fans 14 and under get a coupon for a free hot dog and small Pepsi. Plus, nine lucky kids each Sunday get a chance to take the field with their favorite Royals for pregame introductions during the Dodge Honorary Lineup. After Sunday afternoon home games, all fans can run the bases. Those under 14 are also eligible for membership in the Blue Crew Youth Fan Club, which includes an embroidered baseball cap, two game tickets and the opportunity to be in the front of the line for the Sunday afternoon "fun run."

The best chance your child has of getting players' autographs is on designated autograph nights. Dodge Buck Night is also a great time to take the family out to the ballpark, as hot dogs, peanuts and small Pepsi's are just $1 each all night long. Be sure to stop by the Little K and the Cool Crest Putting Diamond located beyond right field for some big league fun! **Ages: All.**

Kauffman Stadium Tours: 816-504-4222. A guided tour of the stadium includes the Royals Hall of Fame, press box, indoor hitting and pitching facilities and the Royals dug-out. Daily tours start the first Monday in June and continue through the last Friday in August. Tours are not available on legal holidays or day games. **Fee. Ages: 4 and up.**

Kansas City T-Bones Baseball Club, 1800 Village West Parkway, Kansas City, KS, 66111, 913-328-BALL (2255), www.tbonesbaseball.com**.** New to the Kansas City sports scene in 2003, this Independent League team specializes in the family experience of baseball. A kids play area in right field and the crazy antics of Sizzle the mascot keeps younger children entertained. A specially-designed concession stand with lower counters and lower prices makes kids feel at home. Parents love the family restrooms and the Wednesday Family Night special prices.

Kansas City Wizards, Two Arrowhead Drive, Kansas City, MO 64129, 816-920-9300, www.kcwizards.com**.** Fun is the main objective of the Kansas City Wizards, whose season runs from April to November. The club offers several youth soccer programs that combine instruction with tickets to a Wizards game. Encourage your child's soccer team to attend a Wizards game and ask about group ticket prices. Then during the game be sure to watch the matrix scoreboard for your team's name to appear.

Have your team "Play Like the Pros" and play a 15-minute game on the Arrowhead Stadium field prior to a Wizards game. Your kids can also celebrate their birthday with the Wizards with a party in the Pavilion at Arrowhead before any Wizards home game. The Wizards also offer a number of summer camps and clinics throughout the Kansas City area all summer long.

TRIVIA

SOMETIME WHEN YOUR CHILDREN ARE TALKING ABOUT THE SCHOOL CAFETERIA, REMIND THEM THAT FOOD WAS FIRST SERVED IN WHAT IS NOW KNOWN AS CAFETERIA STYLE IN A YMCA HERE IN KANSAS CITY IN 1891.

UMKC Kangaroos, University of Missouri at Kansas City, 5100 Rockhill Rd., 201 SRC, Kansas City, MO 64110, 816-235-TEAM (8326) (tickets), 816-235-1036 (sports information office), www.umkckangaroos.com. UMKC athletes participate in 16 Division I sports, including soccer, golf, volleyball, rifle and more. Among the more popular sports is basketball. Men's games are played at Municipal Auditorium 13th and Central in downtown Kansas City. Women's games are played at Swinney Recreation Center on Campus. A great way to expose your children to the variety of sports offered at UMKC is to join Kasey's Kids Club for children 3-13. Kasey the Kangaroo, the team mascot, will send your children letters and birthday cards, as well as tickets to the game and a T-shirt with his image on it. Find out more about the Kids Club and all of the UMKC sporting activities on the Kangaroos website. **Ages: All.**

WHY KANGAROOS?

UMKC IS AMONG THE MOST UNIQUE MASCOT NAMES IN NCAA DIVISION I SPORTS. THE KANGAROOS GOT THEIR NAME IN 1936 WHEN THE UNIVERSITY ASKED FOR PUBLIC INPUT ON THE NAME OF ITS SPORTS TEAM. ABOUT THE SAME TIME, THE KANSAS CITY COMMUNITY HAD BECOME ENAMORED WITH THE KANSAS CITY ZOO'S ACQUISITION OF TWO BABY KANGAROOS, SO UMKC BECAME THE KANGAROOS. A STRUGGLING YOUNG ARTIST IN KANSAS CITY AT THE TIME DREW ONE OF THE FIRST RENDITIONS OF THE MASCOT USED IN PUBLICATION. THAT ARTIST'S NAME WAS WALT DISNEY.

Young American Bowling Alliance (YABA) of Greater Kansas City, 6025 Raytown Rd., Raytown, MO 64133, 816-358-5460 or 816-358-5470, www.gkcmob.com. The Young American Bowling Alliance is the premier international youth organization in the sport of tenpin bowling. YABA provides opportunities for personal development of youth through bowling and its SMART program and scholarships. YABA gives young bowlers a chance to compete for more than $3 million annually in college scholarships. **Ages: 4 and up.**

VOLUNTEER OPPORTUNITIES

Participating in community service with your child is a wonderful activity and an opportunity to teach empathy, compassion and understanding for others of various cultures, socioeconomic levels and physical capabilities. Volunteer opportunities abound through religious outlets, schools and civic organizations. Many local newspapers list seasonal and specific volunteer needs. Some you may consider that have opportunities for children accompanied by their parents include:

Adopt-A-Highway. This program helps keep our state roadways free of litter and debris. A family may adopt a portion of a highway in your community. Four times a year, you will be expected to walk that section of roadway picking up trash with state supplied materials. Children must be at least eight years old in Missouri and eleven years old in Kansas and under adult supervision. The state will post a sign with your family's name on your section of the highway.

Missouri	816-622-0420
Kansas	913-677-5963

American Red Cross, 211 W. Armour Blvd., Kansas City, MO 64111, 816-931-6662, ext. 250, www.kcredcross.org**.** Blood drives are common events where families can work together serving cookies and other treats. Kids may also enjoy volunteering at any of several water safety programs and fundraisers throughout the year.

Bridging The Gap, 435 Westport Rd., Kansas City, MO 64111, 816-561-1090, www.bridgingthegap.org**.** If teaching your children about caring for the environment is important in your household, this organization needs helps with recycling programs, litter pick-up and office services. The group also participates in ecological restoration projects and an Earth Day walk each spring. You'll find volunteers at many public events passing out literature and picking up recyclable materials.

Christmas Stores. Several area agencies operate stores during the holidays for low-income families to purchase toys and clothing at a reduced price. These are wonderful volunteer opportunities for middle and high school students. Consider hosting a neighborhood party where guests bring gifts for the store or conduct a collection of personal care or food items. For additional ideas and needs, call:

Clay County	816-630-0037
Independence	816-254-4100
Johnson County	913-341-4342
Platte County	816-858-5153
Wyandotte County	913-281-3388

City Union Mission, 1110 E. 11th St., Kansas City, MO 64106, 816-474-9380, ext. 1459, www.cumission.org**.** Young people and families are encouraged to coordinate local drives to provide items needed throughout the year. Review the Drives and Events pages of the website and choose one or two of the listed drives to benefit the poor and homeless.

Foreign Exchange Students. What better way to teach your children about another culture than hosting a foreign exchange student in your home for a few months. Each school district has preferred agencies to work with, so call your school district's administrative offices to learn which organizations they suggest and how to be in touch.

Foster Parenting. Teach your children empathy for children in less fortunate home situations by making your home a foster home. Foster families provide a safe and supportive environment in which the child's emotional, physical and social needs can be met. In Missouri, call the Division Family Support and Children at 816-889-2000. In Kansas, the program is coordinated by Kaw Valley Services at 913-322-4900.

WORRIED ABOUT YOUR TEENAGERS DRINKING? VISIT WWW.THECOOLSPOT.GOV.

Habitat for Humanity. This organization is well-known for building affordable housing for low-income families. While much of the work is skilled, labor-intensive construction, children may help in preparing and serving meals to volunteer workers or other cleanup tasks around the property. Call individual organizations for specific needs.

Eastern Jackson County	816-461-6551
Johnson & Wyandotte	913-342-3047
Kansas City	816-924-1096
Northland	816-468-7190
Truman Heritage	816-461-6551

Harvesters, the Community Food Network, 3801 Topping, Kansas City, MO 64129 816-929-3091. Hold your child's birthday party at Harvester's, with guests bringing canned goods instead of presents. They'll get to tour the warehouse and sort canned goods. Otherwise, your family may volunteer together sorting and repackaging donated food items for needy families. Helps is needed six days a week.

Heart Forest, c/o Greater Kansas City Community Foundation, 1055 Broadway, Kansas City, MO 64105, 816-842-0944. Once each spring and again in the fall, volunteers are needed for a planting day at the Heart Forest, a 22-acre project located southwest of KCI Airport as a symbol of the region's commitment to environmental rejuvenation. The workdays provide a lot of fun, including kite-flying contests, cook-outs and more.

Kansas City Community Gardens, 816-931-3877. Help low-income families grow fresh fruits and vegetables in more than 1,000 vacant lots around the city.

Kansas City Public Library, 816-701-3400, ext 2405. Kids and parents may work together throughout the year sorting books at the Central Library location, 14 W. 10th St., for the annual Friends of the Library Book Sale each autumn.

Lakeside Nature Center, 816-513-8960. Parents and older children can also be a part of the center's volunteer activities that include the care and feeding of injured animals, such as bald eagles and bobcats.

Reach Out and Read Kansas City, 913-588-2793. You know that reading to your children helps develop vocabulary and improve school readiness, so why not to other children at the same time? This early literacy program needs volunteers to model interactive reading techniques for parents and children at 32 low-income clinics around the metropolitan area. Donated books are also needed at these sites.

Special Olympics of Metropolitan Kansas City, 1 Lee Drive, Merriam, KS 66202, 913-789-0330, www.somo.org**.** Special Olympics is a year-round program of sports training and athletic competition for children and adults with mental disabilities. Even the youngest of volunteers can help with water duty and escorting competitors to various events.

The Salvation Army, 3637 W. Broadway, Kansas City, MO 64111, 816-756-1455, www.salvationarmy.org**.** Ringing bells during the holiday season is a great family activity, but this non-denominational Christian organization has need of volunteers throughout the year to raise funds for the needy of our community. Kids can become a pen-pal with senior citizens, make gifts for children at shelters, and bake cookies for food shelters.

Volunteer Center of Johnson County, 913-341-1792. This center coordinates services for organizations and programs throughout Johnson County. Give them a call to see where your family is needed most.

Wayside Waifs, 3901 Martha Truman Rd., Grandview, MO 64137, 816-761-8151, www.waysidewaifs.org**.** This shelter for lost and abandoned pets welcomes family volunteers in dog walking, kennel cleaning and a number of other activities. **Ages: 13 and older.**

FOR MORE INFORMATION ON HOW TO PREVENT CHILDHOOD POISONINGS, VISIT WWW.POISONPREVENTION.ORG.

READING WITH YOUR CHILDREN

Books to Grow, 913-261-2343. This award-winning program is part of the Johnson County Library, but is open to anyone throughout the metropolitan area. The program is a series of coordinated kits for children preschool through 1st grade that include books, audio and videotapes, and activity folders in more than 50 educational themes, such as Children Around the World, Farms and Weather.

Dial-A-Story, 816-701-3456. A service of the Kansas City Public Library, children may call this number 24-hours a day to hear a three to five minute story read by librarians, professionals and neighbors. Stories change weekly.

Irish Museum and Cultural Heritage Center. Volunteers at this facility in Union Station host regular story times where children may hear many of the fascinating tales of Irish heritage and folklore.

Parents and Children Together, PACT, 816-701-3556. This program through the Kansas City Public Library is designed to encourage preschoolers and their parents to read together. Go to any of the ten branches of the library, pick up a PACT brochure, then choose books to read together. After reading the books, list them on the PACT brochure and then receive a free book to keep.

Reading is Fundamental (RIF), 816-361-3600. In Kansas City, this nation-wide program is coordinated by the Boys & Girls Clubs of Greater Kansas City. RIF motivates children to read for pleasure by providing three free colorful, stimulating books to participants during the school year.

TeenStar. Encourage your teenagers to read the newspaper by making sure they have a copy of *The Kansas City Star* each Thursday. This small section of the paper is written by area teenagers about local issues of interest to teens.

Story Time. Many area bookstores, including Borders and Barnes & Noble, offer special story time programs for children on weekends and throughout the week.

Summer Reading Programs are a standard feature at metropolitan area libraries. Usually lasting about eight weeks, these programs encourage kids to read in the summer and provide entertainment in the form of puppet shows, storytellers, magicians and ventriloquists. Below is a list of the main libraries in several library districts; each has several branches. Contact any for programs closest to you.

Cass County Public Library, 816-884-6223, www.casscolibrary.org

Kansas City, MO Public Libraries, 816-701-3400, www.kcpl.lib.mo.us

Mid Continent Public Libraries, 816-836-5200, www.mcpl.lib.mo.us

Leavenworth Public Library, 913-682-5666, http://skyways.lib.ks.us/library/leavenworth/

North Kansas City Public Library, 816-221-3360, www.northkclibrary.org

Johnson County Public Library, 913-495-2400, www.jcl.lib.ks.mo

Olathe Public Library, 913-764-2259, www.olathe.lib.ks.us

Kansas City, KS Public Library, 913-551-3280, www.kckpl.lib.ks.us

Reading Reptile, 328 W. 63rd St., Kansas City, MO 816-753-0441, www.readingreptile.com**.** The metropolitan area's premiere children's bookstore offers numerous special events to encourage the reading habits of young people.

CELEBRATE READING!

National Library Week – the first week of April
Children's Book Week – the second full week of November

"READ PICTURE BOOKS WITH YOUR BABY AND BE SURE TO SHOW HIM THE PICTURES. WHEN SHE'S OLD ENOUGH TO JOIN IN, LET HER TELL PART OF THE STORY, TOO."

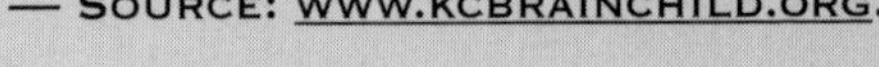

— SOURCE: WWW.KCBRAINCHILD.ORG.

ENTERTAINING PEOPLE & THINGS

Amelia Earhart Show, 816-478-4743. Lesly Lewandowski, an actress and singer, does a one-woman show on the life and accomplishments of the famed aviatrix Amelia Earhart.

Balloonman, 785-865-1404. His kind of super power is making instant toys by twisting balloons into anything you can think of, except a porcupine. Not appropriate for children two or under.

Beth Byrd Productions, 816-305-8188, email: bhahabyrd@comcast.net. In business since 1985, and not much bigger than the children she performs for, Beth offers five different programs for school assemblies. She also clowns and mimes for your special events or creates workshops for your unique interests.

Boomerang Bouncers, 913-962-5969. Choose a purple dragon, a castle, slide or obstacle course for the kids to hop on and in for school events and birthday parties.

Children's Traveling Farm, 816-348-0202. A lamb, a piglet, a calf, a pony and some chicks will gladly come to your birthday party or school event in their very own 27-foot travel trailer. Kids hear stories about how the animals contribute to the human world and receive an activity book. **Ages: 3-9.**

El Grupos Atotonilco, 1015 W. 23rd St., Kansas City, MO 64108, 816-421-1015. This group of adults and children, affiliated with the Guadalupe Center, is available to entertain at parties and other functions with their interpretations of Mexican Folklore.

Klamm Magic, 1412 S. Appleton Ave, Independence, MO 64052, 816-461-4595. This group features Klamm the Magic Man and other magicians and clowns to entertain at parties, special events and school functions.

KRS Magic, 816-331-6155. Kyle Scheel was 13-years-old when he was named Best Magician in KC by the International Brotherhood of Magicians. He can work magic at your event as well.

Bryan Wendling Juggling, 816-561-4695. Chinese yo-yos, hula hoops and glow-in-the-dark stuff are among the many things this guy juggles while climbing up a free standing ladder.

Duane Fields Magic, 816-525-0021, www.duanesmagic.com**.** For more than 30 years, Fields has entertained groups with his sophisticated magic act. Kids like the visuals – colorful props and lots of fire and flash.

Fun Services Midwest, 7803 Meadowview Drive, Shawnee, KS 66227, 913-441-9200, www.funservicesmidwest.com**.** This business does the tough work for you, including setting up a Santa Shoppe or Fun Fair at school and supplying all of the booths, costumes and equipment for a great carnival.

Harmonica Music, 816-587-1117. One of the nation's premiere harmonica players and educators, Phil Duncan loves sharing the history and art of this unique instrument to groups of any size and age.

Imagine Magic, 913-334-2502. You might have seen Gene Hernandez' act at several area restaurants, but he is also available for school parties and events where he dazzles the audience with balloon sculptures, light magic and good-natured teasing.

Jim Cosgrove, 913-219-4815, www.jimcosgrove.com**.** Better known by Kansas City kids as Mr. Stinky Feet, this children's singer/ songwriter performs silly songs about things that kids love – stinky feet, red wagons, and dancing dinosaurs. He's always in demand for performances at schools, libraries, bookstores, and other public events.

Juggling Jeff Walker, 816-792-5559, www.jugglingjeff.com**.** This former elementary teacher has followed his childhood passion for juggling and magic into an entertainment career than includes sculpting zany balloon animals and top spinning. At your party, he will lead group games, provide walk around entertainment and an educational component to the program.

Kids in the Kitchen, 913-710-5171, www.inhomebistro.com**.** For birthday parties, holiday gatherings or play groups, this service comes to your home or day care center with all the equipment and ingredients for a child-size cooking class.

Ko-Arts, 816-931-9545. Members of this group specialize in ethnic dancing and music, including demonstrations and lessons in the Argentine Tango.

Laughing Matters, 913-432-4555, www.leslieandjay.com**.** This husband and wife team does juggling, mime, magic and "other nonsense" for your school parties.

Living Drama, 816-235-2707. This group of professional actors from the Kansas City Repertory Theatre will come to your school with a performance of "A Christmas Carol," and in so doing will teach children what is required in bringing a classic novel to the stage, including set design, scripting, lighting and more.

LuLu Bell the Clown, 913-299-0201, www.ilikeclowns.com**.** LuLu Bell and her friends will paint your face, tell a story, dance with puppets and create balloon art or any other type of fun at your special event.

Marble Lady, 816-587-8687, www.themarblelady.com**.** Considered one of the world's leading authorities on the game of marbles, Cathy Runyan provides energetic and informative programs while teaching the ancient sport to children. She has a permanent display at the Toy and Miniature Museum. *(see listing page 72)*

Mad Science of Greater Kansas City, 10565 Lackman Rd., Lenexa, KS 66219, 913-888-8877, www.madsciencekc.org**.** This imaginative learning program is perfect for sparking an interest in science in children ages 3 -12. All programs, whether for schools, scout troops, summer camps or birthday parties, are correlated to national and state science standards for your age group.

Mascots. Many of our area sports teams and businesses have mascots who make an energetic and fun addition to any event involving children in Kansas City.

Fuzzy the Cosmic Cat - Comets	816-474-2255
Dynamo the Dragon - Wizards	816-920-4733
Kasey the Kangaroo - UMKC	816-235-1036
KC Wolf - The Kansas City Chiefs	816-920-4212
Sluggerrrr - The Kansas City Royals	816-504-4332
Sizzle - The T-Bones	913-328-5622
Victor E. Lane – Kansas Speedway	913-328-3300.

Midwest Storytelling Theater, 816-322-2880. Susansylvia Scott brings her storytelling concerts to your home or school for special occasions. She encourages children to be creative and imaginative as they listen to her folk literature derived from many cultures.

Origami Artists, 816-741-4798. Phil and Betty Jones are retired teachers who provide workshops and entertainment for schools, parties and churches on the Asian art of paper folding.

Paul Mesner Puppets, 816-756-3500, www.paulmesnerpuppets.org**.** For more than 25 years, Paul Mesner has delighted crowds around the world with his theatrical performances that include marionettes and rod puppets. The company also does sock puppet workshops, birthday parties and any number of events.

Rep-Tails, exotic pet mobile, 816-540-5513. This traveling show includes a number of snakes and tortoises, African cats, South American raccoons and chinchillas for kids to hold and touch.

River & Prairie Story Weavers, Box 25261, Kansas City, MO 64119, 816-452-6893, www.storyraps.org**.** This organization represents about 100 professional storytellers who meet twice monthly at locations around the city. Adults and children are invited to listen, observe or participate. The storytellers are available for group presentations for all ages. A Junior Olympics competition invites children 10 and older to tell their stories in a competitive environment.

Stable T Farm for Kids, 913-334-5888. If you want to bring pony, pigs or goats to your school program or birthday party, these are the folks to call. They have Shetland ponies for riding and an unusual creature called a turcken that will be the hit of the program.

Stone Lion Puppetry Theatre, 816-221-5351, www.stonelionpuppets.org**.** This professional puppet theatre is great for preschool through sixth grade with performances including marionettes, shadow, hand and rod puppets. Performances are also offered at the H&R Block City Stage at Union Station.

Tartan, 785-841-7906. This Celtic band has a broad repertoire of Scottish and Irish songs from 600 A.D. to present and provides a wonderful demonstration of Celtic drums and other instruments.

Traditional Music Society, 816-561-1849. This group performs traditional West African and Caribbean drumming, dance and Samba. Teachers are available for short-term and long-term residencies for your school music program.

Traditional Acoustic Music, 816-763-5040. Linda G. Thomas is a retired elementary music teacher with 35 years experience in teaching the hammered dulcimer and other traditional forms of music. She is glad to provide music for pleasure or create an educational program for young people.

Vodill Entertainment Company, 913-648-0011. www.vodvill.com. Richard Renner has been coordinating performances of unique people with useless skills, such as fire-eating and stilt walking, for nearly 25 years. Personally, he does a great vaudeville style act on recycling.

Safety Programs

Healthy Kids University, 816-234-3748. Coordinated through Children's Mercy Hospital, these programs are offered at your request and designed to meet the needs of your group on any health or safety topic.

Kansas City Children's Assistance Network, www.kccan.org. This group of volunteers works to create programs dedicated to the safety and education of children in Kansas City.

Kansas City Missouri Police Department. The Crime Prevention Unit in each patrol division offers safety education programs, including McGruff the Crime Dog, that are available for schools and other groups. Call the appropriate Crime Prevention Unit:

Metro Patrol	816-349-6428
Central Patrol	816-759-6328
East Patrol	816-482-8506
North Patrol	816-437-6229
South Patrol	816-672-2828

Kansas City Power and Light, 816-245-3626, www.kcplkids.com. The metropolitan area's primary energy company offers age-appropriate classroom safety programs for kids beginning in preschool through high school. Among the many activities for kids to get involved in via the website is a billboard coloring contest and college scholarships for those choosing electrical engineering degrees.

QUESTIONS ABOUT YOUR CHILD AND ENVIRONMENTAL HEALTH HAZARDS? CALL 800-421-9916 OR LOG ON TO WWW2.KUMC.EDU/MAPEHSU. THIS SERVICE FROM THE PEDIATRIC ENVIRONMENTAL HEALTH SPECIALTY UNIT AT THE UNIVERSITY OF KANSAS MEDICAL CENTER PROVIDES 24-HOUR INFORMATION ABOUT ANYTHING FROM HOUSEHOLD MOLDS TO CHEMICAL SPILLS. THIS IS ONE OF ONLY 13 SUCH FACILITIES IN THE CONTINENTAL UNITED STATES.

ODDS & ENDS DRAWER

These are some neat things we found, but didn't know where to list them in the book, so other than overlook them, they are here in the odds and ends drawer. Surely you have a drawer like this in your home as well, filled with useful, important stuff that just doesn't fit anywhere else.

Greater Kansas City Mother of Twins Club, 816-943-2111, www.gkcmotc.ourfamily.com**.** This group of mothers who have given birth to multiples, or are expecting to deliver multiples, meets on the second Monday of each month at the St. Joseph Health Center to plan activities and provide support.

LEARN Homeschoolers Association, 913-383-7888, www.kclearn.org**.** Not affiliated with any religious organization, this group provides activities, discounts, information and support to families who choose to homeschool for educational reasons.

National Center for Fathering, 10200 West 75th Street, #267, Shawnee Mission, KS 66204, 913-384-4661, www.fathers.com**.** Located in metro KC, this center was developed by a local dad to help other fathers become more involved in their children's lives. The website provides daily tips for fathers with children in all stages of life. The center also provides programs about fatherhood for schools and community groups.

Passport to Adventure, 816-983-3730. Several area museums, historic sites and nature centers team up each year to create a treasure hunt that offers prizes after kids and families visit the site and answer a few questions. Some of the past participants include the National Frontier Trails Center, Wonderscope Children's Museum and the Ernie Miller Nature Center. The treasure hunt season kicks off on the last Sunday in April at a rally at Science City and continues through September. Passports are found at all participating sites.

The ParentLink Network helps Missouri's parents provide safe, healthy and nurturing environments for their children. Call 800-552-8522 for answers to parenting questions, 8 a.m.-5 p.m., Monday-Friday. Or visit on-line at http://outreach.missouri.edu/parentlink/

Kansas State University Extension service also offers a website with information on managing family relationships. Visit http://www.oznet.ksu.edu and click on "Home, Family and Youth."

Radio Disney, 1190AM, 816-421-1900. This family-friendly radio station presents programming at a level appropriate for elementary and middle school kids with lots of contests and news that children enjoy.

CALENDAR OF EVENTS

Father of the Year Essay Contest, 913-384-4661 or www.fathers.com/contest. Encourage your kids to build their writing skills by entering this contest co-sponsored by the Kansas City Royals and the National Center for Fathering. Awards are made on Father's Day, but entry forms are available in January.

Martin Luther King Day Celebrations. Kansas City hosts one of the largest King Day tributes in the United States. While several smaller communities, neighborhoods and churches offer a variety of programs, Kansas City KS begins with a Motorcade for Hunger, which is a parade that collects food for the needy, and concludes by awarding scholarships to Wyandotte County high school seniors. Call 913-573-5730.

On the Missouri side, musical and dramatic presentations take place in a variety of city locations, but kids will especially enjoy a festival that honors Dr. King's vision for their future. Call 816-241-0404 for details.

Valentine's Day at Lanesfield School, 913-893-6645. Here's a place where kids can make a Valentine and learn how the holiday was celebrated by children a century ago.

Family Magic Show, 913-722-0039. One Saturday afternoon each February, the Roeland Park Community Center invites families to participate in or just sit back and enjoy as professional magicians present a program suitable for any age group.

Black History Month Celebrations. Several museums and community centers coordinate displays on the contributions of African-Americans to the Kansas City region during this month. Some to consider are:

Wyandotte County Museum – 913-721-1078
Bruce R. Watkins Cultural Heritage Center – 816-784-4444
Negro Leagues Baseball Museum – 816-221-1920
Black Archives of Mid-America – 816-483-1300

Snake Saturday Parade, North Kansas City, 816-421-4438. This family-oriented Irish celebration is held on the Saturday before St. Patrick's Day and raises money for Northland charities.

St. Patrick's Day Parade, 816-931-7373. One of the largest parades in the country, this one winds itself throughout downtown with a kaleidoscope of music, floats and parade entries.

Irish Potato Planting, Wyandotte County Museum, 913-721-1078. Teach children the history of the Irish people who suffered through the potato famine by planting potatoes in the museum's heritage garden.

Easter Egg Hunts. Several community centers and church groups coordinate Easter egg hunts for children. Some of them are:

Roeland Park Community Center, 913-722-0039
George Owens Nature Park, 816-257-1760
Jackson County Parks & Recreation, 816-795-8200.

Civil War on the Border, 913-971-5111. Held at the Mahaffie Stagecoach stop the third weekend in April, this reenactment includes a wedding, barn dance and religious services from the period, as well as battles, music and food.

Cherry Blossom Festival, 913-971-6263. Olathe is a little more beautiful this time of year because of the gift of 200 cherry trees to the Olathe Rotary Club from a Rotary Club in Japan. This festival on the third Saturday of the month in Calamity Line Park celebrates the Sakura or cherry blossom, the national flower of Japan.

May Day Festival, 913-893-6645. At the Lanesfield School in Edgerton, celebrate a traditional May Day by dancing around a May Pole and fill a May basket with flowers while enjoying traditional folk music and refreshments.

Cinco de Mayo. This celebration of Mexico's victory over the French in the battle of Puebla in 1862 is recognized in events throughout the city. A couple of good ones are at the Guadalupe Center (816-421-1015) or through Independence Parks and Recreation (816-325-7360).

Harry's Hay Days, Truman Corners Shopping Center, Grandview, 816-763-3900. Live entertainment, fun and games celebrate the birth of President Harry Truman, who lived on a Grandview farm from 1906-1917. There's also a carnival and petty zoo.

Abdallah Shrine Rodeo, 913-788-7898. Held on the grounds of the Wyandotte County Fairgrounds over Memorial Day weekend, this event includes a carnival for the kids and lots of fun events.

Turkey Creek Festival, 913-722-7750. This event in Merriam's Antioch Park starts with a pancake breakfast and includes a petting zoo, hands-on arts and crafts for the kids, paddleboat rides and more.

Kids Fishing Rodeo, 913-438-7275. Sponsored by Johnson County Parks and Recreation, this event at the Shawnee Mission Park Marina is open to kids 12 and under.

Fishing Derby, George Owens Nature Park, Independence, 816-325-7115. Prizes are awarded for the child who catches the most fish and the biggest fish, and all participants ages 5 to 12 get to make their own fish-print T-shirt.

Fishing Derby, Rotary Park, Blue Springs, 816-228-0137. Kids from all over the metro may participate in this event for catfish and blue gill. Lots of prizes for those ages 5 to 14.

Hot Dog and Ice Cream Days, 913-721-1075. At the Agriculture Hall of Fame in Bonner Springs the third weekend in June, you and your kids will receive these two agriculture products for free while touring the living history farm and riding the train around Farm Town.

Parkville Jazz & Fine Arts River Jam, 816-505-2227. This two-day event is held the third weekend in June in the beautiful English Landing Park. Bring a blanket and enjoy nationally-acclaimed music, as well as food and crafts.

Fiesta Bullwhacker, 913-971-5111. The fourth weekend of the month is the biggest family event at the Mahaffie Farmstead in Olathe, including stagecoach rides, historical reenactors, music and lots of activities for the kids.

Slavic Festival, Sugar Creek, 816-252-4400. The rich Slavic heritage of this community is celebrated with dancing, entertainment and food, such as cabbage rolls and Povatica. Special games and dance lessons for the kids are a part of the fun.

Old Shawnee Days, 913-248-2360. This three-day festival celebrates the settlement of Shawnee. Kids enjoy the stick horse rodeo, carnival and baby contest.

Vaile Fancy Faire and Strawberry Festival, 816-325-7111. A strawberry ice cream contest, puppet show and buggy rides top off the entertainment at the Vaile Mansion in Independence. A children's corner hosts activities to acquaint children with the Victorian era.

Heart of America Shakespeare Festival, 816-531-7728, www.kcshakes.org**.** Free performances of Shakespeare's works under the stars in Southmoreland Park, 47th and Oak, is a perfect way to introduce the kids to Shakespeare and enjoy a pleasant summer evening together. The festival sponsors a poster contest for elementary kids in the spring.

Wiener Dog Nationals, 913-299-9797. Held at the Woodlands race track in KCK, this hysterical event tests the speed of 64 dachshunds, better known as wiener dogs.

Independence Day at Lanesfield School in Edgerton, 913-893-6645. Celebrate an old-fashioned Fourth of July with an ice cream social, fireworks and reading of the Declaration of Independence.

Independence Day in Independence, 816-325-7111. Annual event with free family-friendly concert on the grounds of the Mormon Visitors Center. Fireworks follow the show. Bring blankets and lawn chairs.

Platte County Fair, 816-431-3247. The oldest continuously running fair west of the Mississippi provides old-fashioned entertainment for four days just a few miles north of the KCI Airport.

Gladstone Theatre in the Park, 816-436-2200, www.gladstone.mo.us**.** Children are always the stars of the show in the annual productions in July and August in Oak Grove Park, 76th and N. Troost. Check the website for performance times and dates.

Ethnic Enrichment Festival, 816-513-7593. Held in Swope Park, more than 50 ethnic groups from around the world share their food, crafts, folk dance and music the third weekend in August.

Johnson County Fair, 913-856-8860. Goat milking, a greased pig contest and 4-H competitions are among the family fun at the week-long event held at the fairgrounds in Gardner the second week of the month.

Battle of Lone Jack Civil War Reenactment, 816-697-8833. Held the weekend closest to August 16, this event reenacts a five-hour battle of hand-to-hand combat here in 1862.

Lenexa Spinach Festival, 913-541-8592. This annual event commemorates the 1930s when Lenexa was known as the "spinach capital of the world." There's entertainment, arts and crafts, and, of course, a visit from Popeye.

Plaza Art Fair, www.countryclubplaza.com. A children's workshop that includes puppetmaking and other hands on projects is a part of this popular art fair on the Country Club Plaza.

Santa-Cali-Gon Festival, 816-325-7111. This Labor Day weekend festival in Independence celebrates the days of the Santa Fe, California, and Oregon Trails with crafts, entertainment and other activities.

IrishFest, 816-561-7555. Held at Crown Center, the Kansas City Irish Fest is full of Celtic music, dancing, food, drink, heritage displays and a place where children can receive the name of an Irish Pen Pal.

Johnson County Old Settlers Days, 913-782-5551. The weekend after Labor Day fills downtown Olathe with carnival rides, antique cars, a parade and music.

Jesse James Festival, 816-628-4229. Throughout Jessie James' hometown of Kearney, arts and crafts, a rodeo, parade, carnival and period reenactments celebrate the period.

Blue Springs Fall Festival, 816-228-6322. This three day street festival features 300 arts and crafts booths, entertainment and refreshments. A children's area provides games, a carnival, pony rides and a pet parade on Saturday morning.

Renaissance Festival, 800-373-0357, www.kcrenfest.com. Weekends throughout September and October draw a crowd to one of the country's best-known ren fests, which includes Highland Games, Irish music, minstrels, storytellers and lots of fun for the whole family.

Louisburg CiderFest, 913-837-5202. The last week in September and first week in October, the apple cider season gets underway with a festival filled with pumpkins, hayrides and other entertainment.

Apple Fest, 816-640-2909. The apple orchards surrounding Weston come alive with apple butter cooking, cider pressing, a parade and demonstration of old-time arts.

Fall Farm Festival, 913-721-1075. Watch the harvest throughout the fall season on the grounds of the Agriculture Hall of Fame in Bonner Springs.

Gladfest, 816-436-4523. The streets of Gladstone are filled with a parade, arts and crafts, a Kid's Corner and carnival the first weekend of the month.

Snoopy's Pumpkin Patch, Crown Center, 816-274-8444. Snoopy hosts this Halloween event that benefits UNICEF. For a $1 donation, kids can select their own pumpkin from the patch and decorate it on the spot. There's entertainment, a carnival and games to add to the fun.

Magic Woods, Lakeside Nature Center, 816-513-8960. Held on the second full weekend of the month, the nature trail here becomes filled with costumed bird characters who tell stories about their experiences in the Magic Woods.

Missouri Town 1855 Fall Festival, 816-795-8200, ext. 1260. This festival at Fleming Park in Blue Springs includes period dancers and musicians, period games and historic reenactments, and arts and crafts demonstrations.

The Mayor's Christmas Tree Lighting, Crown Center, 816-274-8444. The Friday immediately following Thanksgiving, this lighting ceremony kicks off the campaign to raise money for needy persons in the area. In addition to Christmas caroling and other festivities, make it a family tradition to purchase a wooden ornament made from the wood of the previous year's tree.

A CHILD'S BRAIN DEVELOPS MOSTLY IN THE WORLD, NOT IN THE WOMB. GET OUT AND DISCOVER THE WORLD WITH YOUR CHILD!

American Royal Livestock, Horse Show and Rodeo, 816-221-9800, www.americanroyal.com. Since 1899, the nation's largest combined livestock show and rodeo has attracted competitors from around the country who take part in one of Kansas City's most famous traditions. Also featured are concerts, a grand parade, western show and barbecue contest.

Plaza Lights, 816-753-0100. Thousands of people fill the Country Club Plaza on Thanksgiving night for the lighting of more than 45 miles of lights. The event has been a family tradition in Kansas City since the 1920s. Every year, a child from the audience throws the switch.

Pioneer Christmas, Old Shawnee Town, 913-248-2360. The first Saturday of the month brings carriage rides, Santa Claus, a tree lighting ceremony, entertainment and prizes in an old-fashioned celebration.

Christmas on the River, Parkville, MO, 816-741-7676. The Friday night of the first weekend in December draws more than 10,000 people to this Northland river town for a 1,000 voice choir, fireworks, horse-drawn buggy rides in the park and the arrival of Santa Claus.

Snowflake Festival, 816-561-3737. Each year, the Kemper Museum celebrates the joys of winter at its Snowflake Festival in December. Children and adults are entertained through a variety of activities, from art making to gallery games and free performances.

Christmas in the Park, Longview Lake Park, 816-795-8200, ext. 1225. Three hundred thousand lights and 175 animated figures transform Longview Lake Park into an enchanting winter wonderland.

Jackson County

Downtown Kansas City, North End, Northeast and West Side

Welcome

Convention and Visitors Bureau of Greater Kansas City, 1100 Main St., #2200, Kansas City, MO 64105, 816-221-5242, www.visitkc.org**.**

Transportation

The Max, 816-346-0216, www.kcata.org**.** The Metro Area Express is a rapid transit line that connects the River Market, downtown, Crown Center and the Plaza with fast, frequent and easy-to-use all day service.

Assistance

Guadalupe Center, Inc. 1711 Broadway, Kansas City, MO 64108, 816-472-5108, www.guadalupecenters.org**.** The center's bilingual preschool features an English/Spanish curriculum for students. After-school and school supplement programs for children K through 5th grade features reading, math, computer and science classes. There are reading improvement courses for 7th to 9th graders as well as after-school programs for children K though 8th grade. Tutorials in math, English and job skills for at-risk youth are also part of the center's educational focus, which is open to children of all ethnic backgrounds.

Mattie Rhodes Counseling Center, 1740 Jefferson, Kansas City, MO 64108, 816-471-2536, www.mattierhodes.org**.** In addition to providing individual, family and group therapy for a variety of emotional needs, Mattie Rhodes provides a hands-on creative arts center for parents and children to work together creating projects. Services are offered in Spanish and English. A gallery at 919 W. 17th St. (816-221-2349) displays the work of local Hispanic artists. A satellite counseling center is located at 5001 Independence Ave. (816-241-3780).

Parents as Teachers, (PAT) 120 N. Cedar, Independence, MO 64052, 816-418-4315. The Fairmount Center is one of three centers for the Kansas City School District's district-wide program that features private visits with parent-educators as well as group meetings with other parents. Parents have access to a toy lending library and resource center. Vision, hearing and physical development evaluation screenings are an important and free part of the program. Parents can take advantage of the pre-natal brain development strategies and children's learning opportunities to help their children thrive. **Ages: pre-natal to 5.**

Whatsoever Community Center, 1201 Ewing, Kansas City, MO 64126, 816-231-0227, www.whatsoevercc.org**.** Life skills are the major focus at this center that has been serving the northeast area since 1915. For kids, before and after-school care, pre-school programs, counseling, nutrition classes and a gardening club are popular activities. Tutoring and computer skills classes are also available. A game room and a gym are used for movies and the legendary Whatsoever Boxing Club. **Ages: 3 and up.**

Community Centers

Don Bosco Community Center, 531 Garfield Ave., Kansas City, MO 64124, 816-691-2900. Equipped with a gym and game room, the center offers field trips, special activities and events for youngsters. Don Bosco also partners with Youthnet for after school fitness programs for kids of all ages. Summer camp runs all summer with mini-camps focusing on everything from cheerleading to soccer to computers. **Ages: 6 and up.**

Kansas City Parks and Recreation Community Centers, 816-513-7500, www.kcmo.org. Arts and crafts, sports and fishing, piano, tennis and chess are just a few of the offerings by the following community centers as part of their activities for children and families:

Garrison Community Center, 1124 E. 5th St., 816-784-1140
Gregg/Klice Community Center, 1600 John "Buck" O'Neil Way, 816-784-1135
Tony Aguirre Community Center, 2050 West Penway, 816-784-1300

THE GREAT OUTDOORS

Kansas City Missouri Parks and Recreation Department, 4600 E. 63rd St., Kansas City, MO 64130, 816-513-7500, www.kcmo.org. Most area parks offer picnic areas, ballfields, tennis courts, playgrounds, shelters and bathrooms. Call the Kansas City Missouri Parks and Recreation Department for specific requests. Otherwise, these are some of our favorites:

Kessler Park, The Paseo to Belmont Blvd, North Bluffs. A nice biking trail for parents and kids runs almost four miles through this park that is popular for kite flying in the summer and sledding in the winter. Included in the park is Indian Mound, where remains of American Indians have been discovered. North Terrace Lake is popular for fishing. Across from the park is a nice observation point of the Missouri River valley. Adjacent is the Concourse, a mini-park in itself with shelters and a sprayground fountain for children to play in during warm weather months.

Cliff Drive Scenic Byway, The Paseo and Independence Ave. to Gladstone Blvd. This Missouri Scene Byway is four miles long, passing along the edge of Kessler Park and providing an outstanding view of the city. Cliff Drive was built from 1893 to 1915 and is considered one of the country's best examples of early urban planning.

Berkley Park, the riverfront from Heart of America Bridge to the ASB Bridge. This one-mile long esplanade provides a paved walking, jogging path atop the levee overlooking the Missouri River. Owned by the Port Authority, but managed by Kansas City Missouri Parks and Recreation, the 1000 acres of Berkley Park is connected to the River Market at 5th and Main and is the site of numerous festivals and special events.

THINGS TO DO

Airline History Museum, 201 N.W. Lou Holland Dr., Hangar 9., Kansas City, MO 64116, 816-421-3401, www.airlinehistorymuseum.com. Located at the downtown airport and operated entirely by volunteers, this museum relives the glamour days of propeller-driven aircraft that first crossed the Atlantic Ocean and rounded the globe. Lockheed's Super Constellation, the Connie, is the anchor of this museum. **Ages: 5 and up. Fee.**

American Jazz Museum, 1616 E. 18th St., Kansas City, MO 64108, 816-474-8463, www.americanjazzmuseum.com. Located where it all started in the historic 18th and Vine Jazz District, this interactive museum lets kids explore a working recording studio and sound library. The Wee-Bop Room, designed for children under eight years of age, provides an introduction to jazz through creative activities, such as making your own instrument. In addition, the museum presents a variety of children's programs including jazz storytelling, wee-bop festival, family day and creative arts activities. **Ages: All. Fee.**

American Royal Museum, 1701 American Royal Ct., Kansas City, MO 64102, 816-221-9800, www.americanroyal.com. This museum reminds kids where milk comes from as well as other facts about the role of agri-business in our lives through interactive exhibits and displays. School tours are offered year-round. Tours during the American Royal include show arenas, the Petting Zoo and the World of Agriculture. There are special children's performances, including a Youth Invitational Rodeo. Call for summer class schedules. **Ages: preschool and up. Fee.**

Arabia Steamboat Museum, 4th and Grand in the City Market area, Kansas City, MO 64106, 816-471-1856, www.1856.com. In 1856, the Arabia Steamboat sank in the Missouri River near Parkville and in 1988, it was uncovered under 45 feet of mud in a Kansas cornfield with all of its cargo intact. Kids can watch as employees restore old boots, buggy whips and buckets of nails, but they always get excited about the bones of an old mule, the only passenger to perish as the Arabia sank. Organized groups of students may also participate in the restoration of some artifacts and learn about organic preservation techniques. **Ages: 6 and up. Fee**.

Big River Tours, 816-470-3206, www.bigrivertours.com. With capabilities of launching from Kansas City Riverfront Park, just east of the Isle of Capri Casino, this company offers your family a private boat ride along the Missouri River complete with story telling from the days of Lewis and Clark to today. Climb around on sand bars and rock dams, watch wildlife in the water, and take a look at the underside of our bridges. Bring a picnic and snacks. Restrooms available. Lifejackets provided. **Ages: All. Fee.**

Charles Evans Whitaker U.S. District Court, 400 E. 9th St., Kansas City, MO 64106, 816-512-5016. This 2 1/2 hour tour includes presentations by several law enforcement agencies, a chance for kids to sit in the jury box or witness stand, and even be handcuffed. You must schedule tours three weeks to a month in advance. **Ages: 4th grade and up. Free.**

City Market, Main and 5th St., Kansas City, MO 64106, 816-842-1271, www.kc-citymarket.com. A bustling Saturday morning farmers' market offers cooking classes and a number of seasonal, fun activities along with fresh produce. Sunday's market includes arts and crafts. The City Market is the site of numerous concerts and special events for families throughout the year. **Ages: All.**

Comedy City, 300 Charlotte, Kansas City, MO 64106, 816-842-2744, www.comedycity.cc. Competitions between two teams of comedians create hilarious fun for the entire family just east of the River Market area. Audience participation makes each night a different experience. Teams from Comedy City are also available for programs at school. Summer stand-up comedy classes are a good opportunity for your budding star. **Ages: 5 and up. Fee.**

Creative Candles, 2101 Broadway, Kansas City, MO 64108, 816-474-9711, www.creativecandles.com. Kids get to dip their own "critter candles" at the conclusion of the tour of this candle manufacturing plant that makes more than 45 different colors of candles, some of which are shipped to the White House. Tours are for groups only and require a reservation. **Ages: 6 and up. Fee.**

Federal Reserve Bank, 925 Grand Ave., Kansas City, MO 64198, 816-881-2683, www.kc.frb.org. Visitors see inside the two vaults where money and valuables are stored. See where more than one million checks a day are processed and the high-speed sorter that can count, sort or destroy up to 100,000 bills an hour. Learn the history of U.S. currency and plans for its future. A 15-minute educational video is a part of the two daily tours. A two-week advance reservation is needed, dependent upon national security conditions. **Ages: 14 and up. Free.**

Grace and Holy Trinity Cathedral, 415 W. 13th St., Kansas City, MO 64141, 816-474-8260. Boasting one of the largest mechanical action pipe organs in Missouri, this century-old cathedral hosts a number of musical programs that brings in performers from around the world. These concerts particularly appeal to youngsters with keyboard experience or those with a keen interest in the musical arts. A tour of the cathedral provides an interesting perspective to Kansas City history. **Ages: 10 and up. Free.**

TRIVIA

EVEN THOUGH KANSAS CITY IS NICKNAMED THE COW TOWN, THE CRITTER ON TOP OF THE 60-FOOT TOWER IN MULKEY SQUARE PARK AT 13TH AND SUMMIT IN THE QUALITY HILL AREA, IS A BULL. HE DOESN'T HAVE A NAME, BUT THE19-FOOT LONG BULL ORIGINALLY ADORNED THE AMERICAN HEREFORD ASSOCIATION BUILDING IN THAT NEIGHBORHOOD, BUT WHEN A NEW COMPANY MOVED INTO THE BUILDING, THE BIG BULL GOT A NEW SPOT ON WHICH TO WATCH THE COMINGS AND GOINGS IN COW TOWN.

Heritage Hikes, 816-235-1448. Take a walk through one of our three downtown neighborhoods with a tour guide from the Historic Kansas City Foundation who brings to life some of the buildings and activities from Kansas City's earliest days. The hike is about three miles and lasts about three hours. **Ages: maturity counts here, but recommended age is about 10 and up. Fee.**

Historic Elmwood Cemetery, 4900 E. Truman Rd., Kansas City, MO 64127, 816-231-0373, www.historickcelmwood.org**.** Some of the most colorful characters to have passed in – not through – Kansas City in its early days can be found here and a guided tour is both educational and fun for the kids. Stories include tales of Jesse James, Robert E. Lee, the TITANIC, Nabisco, hot dogs, vinegar, Wild Bill Hickok, diamonds, Jayhawkers and taxes. A Haunted Run on Halloween is a fundraiser for the upkeep of this cemetery. **Ages: 8 and up. Free.**

Kansas City City Hall, 414 E. 12th St., Kansas City, MO 64106, 816-513-1313. Highlights of this tour include a visit to city council chambers, a discussion of city government, and a trip to the observation deck (weather and national security conditions permitting). Tours can be arranged for more in-depth issues concerning local government. **Ages: 8 and up. Free.**

Kansas City, MO Fire Department, 635 Woodland Ave., Kansas City, MO 64106, 816-784-9999. The Kansas City Fire Department gives several apparatus demonstrations for schools, block parties, as well as providing fire safety talks for schools and student groups. Dial ext. # 1 for the fire truck demonstration. Ask about the Kids' Safety House, a custom-designed trailer that includes a living room, kitchen and child's bedroom complete with fire alarms, smoke simulators and heated door sensors. Dial ext. # 4 for the Kids' Safety House demonstration. **Ages: 5 and up. Free.**

Kansas City Fire Museum, 1019 Cherry St., Kansas City MO, 64106, 816-474-0200, www.kcfiremuseum.com**.** Located in the former Firestation # 10, built in 1909, this small museum has an interactive area where kids can play with fire hoses and fire hydrants. Two antique ladder trucks and other fire equipment are on display. Open on Friday and Saturday only. **Ages: 5 and up. Free.**

Kansas City Museum and Planetarium, 3218 Gladstone Blvd., Kansas City, MO 64123, 816-483-8300, www.kcmuseum.com**.** Originally an ornate 70-room mansion, the museum holds fascinating exhibits of frontier life and early regional history. Displays include replicas of an Osage Indian lodge, flatboat and covered wagon and native animal dioramas. The Planetarium offers seasonal shows that demonstrate how the stars move throughout the year. At the Old Corner Drugstore, you can enjoy an old-fashioned phosphate or ice cream sundae. **Ages: preschool and up. Fee.**

Kansas City Southern Industries, 427 W. 12th St., Kansas City MO 64105, 816-983-1303. The lobby of this transportation business is filled with railroad memorabilia, including a railcar used by Harry Truman during his presidency. **Ages: All. Free.**

Lewis and Clark Point, 8th and Jefferson, Kansas City, MO. A marker and statue commemorates the two and a half year journey by the famed explorers that brought them along the Missouri River to this area. The site overlooks a spectacular view of Kansas City and the joining of the Kaw and Missouri rivers, where the Corps of Discovery camped for three days in June 1804.

Negro Leagues Baseball Museum, 1616 E. 18th St., Kansas City, MO 64108, 816-221-1920, www.nlbm.com**.** A number of interactive displays allow kids the opportunity to explore this important time in American sports history. See the locker rooms and hear the sounds from this era. An indoor ballfield and statues of some of the league's best highlight the tour. **Ages: All. Fee.**

U.S. Post Office, 1700 Cleveland, Kansas City, MO 64121, 816-504-3284. Children learn all of the steps of mail processing from the time they put a letter in the mailbox to the time it's delivered. At the conclusion of the hour-long tour, kids receive a coloring book. **Ages: 8 and up. Free.**

West Bottoms Haunted House, I-35 and 12th St., Kansas City, MO Not just for Halloween, these haunted warehouses open in August and can be rented at other times during the year for special events. **Ages: teen and up. Fee.**

The Catacombs, 816-474-3845, www.deadlydouble.com.
The Beast, 816-842-4280 or 842-0320, www.kcbeast.com
The Edge of Hell, 816-842-4280 or 842-0320, www.edgeofhell.com.

FUN FOOD AND TREATS

Chubby's Breakfast and Burgers, 1835 Independence Ave., Kansas City, MO 64124, 816-842-2482. Take the kids back in time to this 1950s-style restaurant that serves good old-fashioned burgers and ice cream sodas. Kids get a free lollipop to take home.

Have-A-Snack, 2641 Van Brunt Blvd., Kansas City, MO 64128, 816-924-1878. This is a great neighborhood drive-in that serves Italian steak sandwiches along with cheeseburgers, fries and other fun food.

Town Topic, 2013 Broadway, Kansas City, MO 64108, 816-842-2610. This is the original of three legendary Town Topic burger joints in Kansas City. The Sparks family opened this one in 1942 and still serves burgers at those original 13 counter stools to the great grandkids of their first customers. Town Topic is open 24-hours a day, seven days a week.

MIDTOWN

WELCOME

Crown Center Customer Service, 2450 Grand Ave., Kansas City, MO 64108, 816-274-8444, www.crowncenter.com**.**

The Country Club Plaza Association, 4744 Central, Kansas City, MO 64112, 816-753-0100, www.countryclubplaza.com**.**

Westport Community Improvement District, 4050 Pennsylvania, #135, Kansas City, MO 64111, 816-531-4370.

ASSISTANCE

Healthy Kids University, Children's Mercy Hospital, 2401 Gillham Rd., Kansas City, MO 64108, 816-234-3748. Programs are offered at your request and designed to meet the needs of your group on any children's health topic.

Kansas City's Promise, 4510 Belleview, #200, Kansas City, MO 64111, 816-531-9200, www.kcpromise.org**.** This organization coordinates resources for communities to provide children with caring adults, safe places, a healthy start, marketable skills and opportunities to serve. Check the website for age-appropriate lists of activities you can be doing with your child to ensure those factors are present in your child's life.

COMMUNITY CENTERS

Swimming, basketball, judo, pottery, language and summer camps are just a few of the offerings for children and families at the following centers:
Brush Creek Community Center, 3801 Emanuel Cleaver Blvd., Kansas City, MO 64130, 816-784-4000

Westport-Roanoke Community Center, 3601 Roanoke Rd., Kansas City, MO 64111 816-784-5200

THE GREAT OUTDOORS

Discovery Center, 4750 Troost, Kansas City, MO 64110, 816-759-7300, www.kcconservation.com. Lewis and Clark and the Corps of Discovery serve as honorary hosts for this joint project between the Missouri Department of Conservation and the Department of Natural Resources. Located on the ten-acre urban conservation campus in Kauffman Legacy Park, just east of the Country Club Plaza, the center emphasizes learning by doing. Groups may schedule time in one of six workshops to learn outdoor skills and do hands-on activities. Workshops include making bird feeders, cooking fish, game and other edibles, and aquatic studies. Visitors may drop in and tour the environmentally-friendly building and garden, attend special events and obtain conservation information, obtain permits and purchase nature-related items at the Outdoor Missouri Gift Shop. **Ages: All.**

Kansas City Missouri Parks and Recreation Department, 4600 E. 63rd St., Kansas City, MO 64130, 816-513-7500, www.kcmo.org.

SPECIAL AREA PARKS AND PLAYGROUNDS

Most area parks offer picnic areas, ballfields, tennis courts, playgrounds, shelters and bathrooms. Call the Kansas City Missouri Parks and Recreation Department for specific requests. Otherwise, these are some of our favorites:

Mill Creek Park, 47th and Broadway. As home to the famous J. C. Nichols Fountain, Mill Creek Park is certainly the most photographed park in the city. But it is also busy throughout the year because of its rubberized turf one-mile fitness trail, its 12 acres of open space for frisbee and volleyball, and the ecopond, a 15,000 gallon pond that is home to native Missouri plants and waterfall.

Montgall Park Playgound, 22nd & Agnes, behind Children's Mercy Hospital. This wonderful playground is a partnership between the Center for Childhood Safety, Kansas City Missouri Parks and Recreation and many local businesses. The equipment and construction materials make it one of the safest and most modern playgrounds in the city.

Penn Valley Park, 31st and Wyandotte at Broadway. The spring of 2005 witnessed the debut of Kansas City's first outdoor skateboard park in this historic 130 acres across from Union Station and Crown Center. Dog lovers enjoy the park for its three-acre off-leash dog park. Penn Valley also includes tennis courts, ballfields, and a running/jogging/biking path with paved and unpaved sections. As home to the beautiful Liberty Memorial, the famous Scout statue and the Firefighters' Fountain, Penn Valley Park is host to numerous festivals and events all year long.

Pioneer Park, Westport Rd. and Broadway. It's a small park, but worth the stop for historical and educational purposes. There's an in-ground map of the United States during the time of westward expansion, complete with pioneer and explorer routes. There's also a statue of Westport's earliest settlers.

THINGS TO SEE AND DO

Amtrak, 2200 Main Street, Kansas City, MO 64108, 800-872-7245, www.amtrak.com. Take your kids on a train trip, maybe just to the station in Lee's Summit and back. Amtrak also makes stops in some of Missouri's great communities, such as Warrensburg, Sedalia, Jefferson City, Hermann and, of course, St. Louis. What a great weekend outing while introducing your children to the joy of train travel.

Battle of Westport Tour, Westport Historical Society, 4000 Baltimore, Kansas City, MO 64111, 816-561-1821, www.westporthistorical.org. The Battle of Westport took place in October 1864 with about 3,000 casualties over three days. A driving/walking tour covers 32 miles around Kansas City, stopping at 25 descriptive markers. The Westport Historical Society provides free maps and detailed directions. **Ages: 8 and up. Free.**

Harris-Kearney House, 4000 Baltimore, Kansas City, MO 64111, 816-561-1821, www.westporthistorical.org. Built in 1855, this former boarding house was famed throughout the Old West for its hospitality and food. Children can see authentically furnished rooms and learn about early Kansas City history from members of the Westport Historical Society. **Ages: 8 and up. Fee.**

KCPT Channel 19, Public Television, 125 E. 31st St., Kansas City, MO 64108, 816-756-3580, www.kcpt.org. The 45-minute tour of Kansas City's public television station includes the offices, studio and engineering/production room. Cameras are on in the studio so children can see themselves on the monitors. Two weeks notice is needed to schedule a tour. **Ages: 6-17. Free.**

Kansas City Art Institute, 4415 Warwick Blvd., Kansas City, MO 64111, 816-474-5224, www.kcai.edu. This is where Walt Disney received his training in art. Saturday and evening classes are available in a variety of mediums for kids of all ages. **Ages: 6-16.**

Kemper Museum of Contemporary Art, 4420 Warwick, Kansas City, MO 64111, 816-561-3737, www.kemperart.org. Monthly family programs include hands-on activities to introduce children to the concepts of contemporary art. *(See page 12 for more)*. **Ages: All. Free.**

Laugh-O-Gram Studios, 31st and Forest, 816-474-7100, www.laughogram.com. This decrepit building is where a struggling young artist, with so little talent that the *Kansas City Star* wouldn't hire him to draw advertisements, first drew a character he called Mortimer Mouse. The artist was Walt Disney and the mouse became Mickey Mouse. Efforts are underway to restore the building, which will eventually include a theater, Disney-related statues, hands-on exhibits and character statues.

The Learning Exchange, 3132 Pennsylvania, Kansas City, MO 64111, 816-751-4100, www.lx.org. Since 1972, the Learning Exchange has provided stimulating learning resources for children. Although its services are now provided only through organized school groups, Earthworks, a study in environmental education, and Exchange City, an economics and social studies model, remain among the most popular learning tools for children and teachers in metropolitan Kansas City today.

Liberty Memorial and Museum, 100 W. 26th St., Kansas City, MO 64108, 816-784-1918, www.libertymemorialmuseum.org**.** At the northern edge of Penn Valley Park, across the street from Union Station, is the 217-foot memorial honoring those who served the United States during World War I. It is the only such memorial in the United States. The collection includes objects and documents ranging from weaponry and uniforms used during the war, to letters and postcards from the field. One of the more interesting pieces is a Model J 1917 Harley Davidson Army motorcycle. Children may enjoy the elevator ride to the top of the tower. Special programs occur throughout the year. **Ages: 8 and up. Fee.**

Nelson-Atkins Museum of Art, 4525 Oak St., Kansas City, MO 64111, 816-561-4000, www.nelson-atkins.org**.** From the oversized shuttlecocks outside and a stroll through the Henry Moore Sculpture Garden to the expanded exhibits inside, the Nelson is a great place to introduce children to the beauty of art of all styles and sizes. Special events throughout the year are programmed for families to enjoy together. *(see page 13 for more)*. **Ages: All. Free**.

Safety Street, 2401 Campbell, Kansas City, MO 64108, 816-513-6327. It looks like a fun model city with mock storefront and vehicles, but Safety Street offers hands on learning about bicycle, automobile, bus and pedestrian safety. The three-hour program may also include tips on fire safety and hand washing. **Ages: 5-8. Free.**

Thomas Hart Benton Home & Studio, 3616 Belleview, Kansas City, MO 64111, 816-931-5722, www.mostateparks.com/benton.htm**.** Guides lead you on a 45 minute tour through the famed Missouri artist's home where he spent the last half of his life. His studio remains as it was when he worked there from 1939 –75. Children see the artist's work and listen to highlights of Benton's colorful years. **Ages: 5 and up. Fee.**

Union Cemetery, 227 E. 28th Terr., Kansas City, MO 64108, 816-472-4990. The names on the markers in this cemetery are those who helped influence the growth of Kansas City in its early days and forge the western expansion of the United States. Among those buried here is Alexander Majors, who helped start the Pony Express. Self-guided tour brochures are available at the sexton's cottage. **Ages: 8 and up. Free.**

WDAF TV 4, 3030 Summit, Kansas City, MO 64108, 816-753-4567, www.wdaftv4.com. Kansas City's first television station does not give tours of its facilities, but offers a speaker's bureau of TV personalities. Your request must be faxed on organization letterhead one month in advance to 816-932-9221 and include date, time location, length of appearance, speaker's responsibilities, number of people in attendance, contact person, phone number and address.

WHY WAS IT NAMED UNION CEMETERY?
UNION CEMETERY WAS LOCATED IN A RURAL AREA HALF WAY BETWEEN THE TOWN OF WESTPORT AND THE TOWN OF KANSAS WHEN IT WAS DEVELOPED IN 1857. SINCE IT WAS TO BE USED BY BOTH TOWNS, IT WAS CONSIDERED A "UNION" OF THOSE COMMUNITIES.

FUN FOOD

Murray's Ice Cream & Cookies, 4120 Pennsylvania, Kansas City, MO 64111, 816-931-5646. This true homemade ice cream is sure to please even the pickiest of ice cream aficionados. Try the delicious waffle cones dipped in white chocolate and rolled in crushed candies.

Union Station, 30 W. Pershing Rd., Kansas City, MO 64108, 816-460-2020, www.unionstation.org.

Kansas City's Union Station was one of the last monumental train stations built in this country when it opened in 1914. From 1916 through 1919, more than 767,000 service men and women passed through Kansas City's Union Station. All stopped at the Red Cross Canteen on the south end by the telephone booths. Union Station was home to one of Fred Harvey's famous Harvey House Restaurants.

Throughout the 1930s and 40s, Union Station was one of the busiest in the country, but as train travel declined, so did the use and need for Union Station. Amtrak's last train departed the station in 1985 and the doors of Union Station officially closed in 1989.

Union Station was placed on the National Register of Historic Places in 1972 and in 1996, Greater Kansas City made national history when it passed a bi-state 1/8-cent sales tax to fund the renovation of the station and create Science City. This was the first such bi-state tax in the country.

Union Station is today the site of some of the city's most vibrant celebrations and gatherings. In addition to striking architecture and exquisite artistic detail, Union Station is a stimulating educational and entertainment destination that attracts visitors from around the country. It continues to be the place for fun, learning and history. It combines the best of science centers, theme parks, retail and theater into a unique "only in Kansas City" experience.

Docent led tours that explore the architecture and history of Union Station are offered on Saturdays and include characters from the early days of train travel, such as Harvey Girls and Jarvis Hunt, the architect of Union Station. The tour includes details of the 1933 Union Station Massacre, where a shoot-out with gangster Pretty Boy Floyd and others that killed two Kansas City police officers, two FBI agents, and gangster Frank Nash. You can still see the bullet holes outside, east of the main front doors on the eastern end.

The Grand Hall is home to a simple, yet entertaining fountain you have to experience to understand. You and your children can run through the water without getting wet. The Grand Hall is also home to the numerous traveling exhibits that introduce the Kansas City public to some of the most intriguing aspects of our history, our culture and our world.

Science City (www.sciencecity.com) includes numerous interactive learning stations that allow children to dig fossils and come face-to-face with prehistoric creatures that lived in this area more than 65 million years ago or train as an astronaut and fly a mission to Mars. There's a newsroom, a crime lab and a medical center, all encouraging children to explore the science and technology that contribute to these day-to-day aspects of our lives.

The **Union Station Theater District** includes the City Extreme Screen with a five-story screen formatted for two and three-dimensional films. Live theater is available at the H&R Bloch City Stage, which is also home to the Stone Lion Puppet Theatre and other performances.

The **Kansas City Irish Museum and Cultural Center** makes its home on the Theatre level. In addition to genealogy research materials, paintings and books, the Center hosts rotating exhibits on Irish issues from participating museums around the world. Ask about the story times for children to hear many of the fascinating tales of Irish heritage and folklore.

Train Town, located in the Extreme Screen Lobby, includes four model train layouts. These are a Lionel train set and N-scale, O-scale and HO scale. Real train cars are on exhibit outside and train memorabilia is on display throughout Union Station.

While at Union Station, explore the wide variety of offerings for children at **Buster's Bookshelf**, just west of the Clock, or the Station Master store that offers Union Station and train related souvenirs.

Union Station and Science City offer special packages for birthday parties and other events.

Rain or shine, kids enjoy a trip through **The Link,** a walkway that joins Union Station and Crown Center. Enter the Link on the east end of Union Station through the Harvey House Lunchroom, after picking up a bite to eat at one of several eateries available.

Crown Center, 2450 Grand Ave, Kansas City, MO 64108, 816-274-8444, www.crowncenter.com.

This innovative entertainment center was the dream of Joyce C. Hall, the founder of Hallmark Cards. This 85-acre complex is the international headquarters of Hallmark Cards and the site of some of the city's most creative and entertaining events.

Crown Center Square is the place to take the kids to play in the summer. A series of 49 jets spout water up to 25 feet in the air and splash down all over children and others who are welcomed to play in the mist. In the winter, Crown Center Square is home to one of the nation's tallest Christmas trees, the Mayor's Christmas Tree. The lighting ceremony here the night after Thanksgiving is accompanied by singing of carols in a candlelight setting.

The Crown Center Ice Terrace, 816-274-8412, is the city's only public outdoor ice rink, with skating from November through March, seven days a week. Lessons for beginners are offered on Saturday mornings.

Inside, the Crown Center Showplace on Level One, is where many of the exhibits and live performances take place. There's always something happening here.

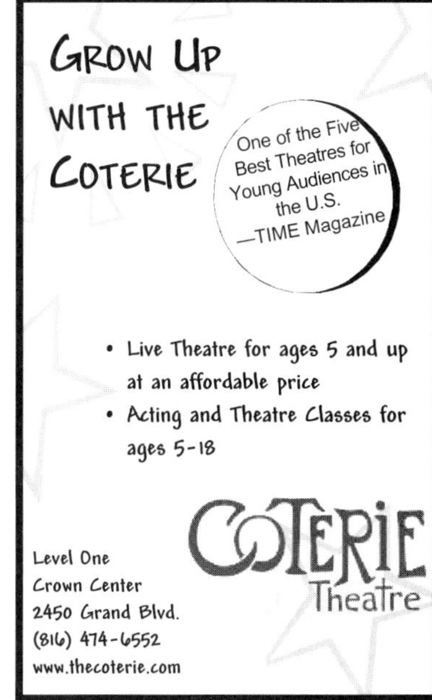

The Coterie Theatre *(see All Around the Town, page 11)* 816-474-6552, combines the excitement of live theatre with positive and educational themes directed at young people and families.

Hallmark Visitors Center, 816-274-5672, tells the story of Hallmark Cards, Inc., beginning with the first boxes of greeting cards sold by Joyce C. Hall from his room at the local YMCA. But kids will love the displays of holiday ornaments, the touching commercials for Hallmark products, and watching the process of cards being printed on the presses. The highlight of the self-guided tour is always the bow-making machine, where kids and adults can make their own bows to take home.

Kaleidoscope, 816-274-8301, is designed especially to stir the creativity of children and is operated at no charge as a gift of the Hallmark employees to the children of the community. With the help of colored paper, crayons, glue, yarn, stickers and a stimulating environment, children are encouraged to go wild and explore their own sense of creative expression. **Ages: 5-12. Free.**

THINGS TO SEE AND DO

Mad Platter, 816-361-6000, located on the second level is a paint-your-own ceramic studio that caters to kids, with lots of fun piggy banks and other treasure boxes. Parents of newborns are often found painting their babies' hands and feet here, then applying the print to a plate or picture frame. **Ages: All. Fee.**

Chip's Chocolate Factory /Kansas City Fudge, Level 2, 816-421-0012. Watching the workers here make the fudge, chocolate and other treats is almost as much fun as eating the results. Tours allow kids to see how different products are made by machine and by hand.

Crayola Café, Level 2, 816-435-4128. If you see people walking around Crown Center with balloons, they may be waiting for their table at this popular restaurant where coloring on your placemat is as much fun as ordering the unique drinks, main courses and fun desserts, which often incorporate the names of Crayola Crayons in the title.

Fritz's Railroad Restaurant, Level 1, 816-474-4004. A fun restaurant to take young and old railroad fans, a burger at this Kansas City tradition is delivered to tables by overhead electric trains. Kids get a paper engineer's hat. The food is just as good at the Crown Center location as at the original Fritz's in Kansas City, KS.

FUN SHOPPING AT CROWN CENTER

Crayola Store, Level 2, 816-274-7500. More than a retail outlet, this store includes a crayon-making demonstration and interactive displays that teach about color and creativity.

Halls Station, Level 3, 816-274-5035. "Just looking" is an expected response to the sales person's offer of assistance at this store where three large model train lay-outs attract people of all ages. Trains, trains and more trains are on display on the walls, and are for sale as well.

Zoom, Level 2, 816-842-8697. Check out the lunch box display around the store that is filled with educational items for kids of all ages.

THE PLAZA

The J.C. Nichols Country Club Plaza, 816-753-0100, www.countryclubplaza.com. Recognized world-wide for its outdoor, public museum quality filled with Spanish architecture, European sculptures and distinctly Kansas City fountains, the Country Club Plaza is one of the most popular destinations for locals and visitors alike throughout the year. Designed in 1922 as the nation's first suburban shopping district, today The Plaza is like taking a mini-vacation to the great cities of Europe. Sir Winston Churchill and wife greet you on the south side of Brush Creek, while replicas of Seville, Spain's most recognizable buildings provide a backdrop for bronze sculptures from Italian artist Donatello Gabrielli. From the Plaza Lights to the Plaza Art Fair, The Plaza is central to all this is Kansas City.

THINGS TO SEE AND DO

Brush Creek Park. One of the defining landmarks of the Plaza, Brush Creek was once a watering hole for pioneers and stagecoaches leaving Westport on the Santa Fe Trail. Today, it is the site of numerous public events and its tree-lined banks are a nice place to walk and let the kids play.

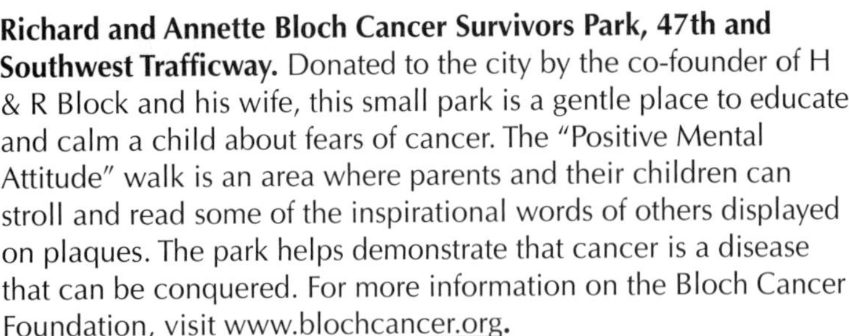

Richard and Annette Bloch Cancer Survivors Park, 47th and Southwest Trafficway. Donated to the city by the co-founder of H & R Block and his wife, this small park is a gentle place to educate and calm a child about fears of cancer. The "Positive Mental Attitude" walk is an area where parents and their children can stroll and read some of the inspirational words of others displayed on plaques. The park helps demonstrate that cancer is a disease that can be conquered. For more information on the Bloch Cancer Foundation, visit www.blochcancer.org.

The Plaza Tennis Center, 4747 J.C. Nichols Parkway, Kansas City, MO 64112, 816-784-5100. The center includes 14 outdoor, lighted courts, a pro shop, café and locker rooms. Permanent bleachers seat about 300 spectators. This is where the Kansas City Explorers (*page 15)* play their matches.

Pride of Kansas City Carriage, Inc., the corner of Nichols and Pennsylvania, 816-531-1999. A carriage ride is a Kansas City tradition.

Surreys Carriage Co, the corner of Nichols and Wyandotte, 816-531-2673. A horse-drawn carriage ride is a fun activity no matter what the season.

Walking Tour of Plaza. An Art and Architecture guide is available at no charge at Plaza Customer Service, 4745 Central.

FUN FOOD ON THE PLAZA

Cherries Frozen Custard Bistro, 428 Ward Parkway, Kansas City, MO 64111, 816-561-6338. This fun place has a unique combination of mixings and entertaining names, such as PB&J custard, Giggles & Wiggles, or Dough-Re-Me. Indoor and outdoor seating are available.

Winstead's, 101 Brush Creek, Kansas City, MO 64112, 816-753-2244. Although Winstead's has several locations around the city, this is the original burger joint that opened in 1940 and is legendary for frosty malts, skyscraper sodas and delectable onion rings. In November, the malts often coincide with flavors available in the national Girl Scout cookies sales.

FUN SHOPS

Discovery Channel, 222 W. 47th St., Kansas City, MO 64111, 816-931-0289. If your family enjoys watching The Discovery Channel, you will enjoy all of the hands-on, educational and fun toys this store has to offer.

Three-Dog Bakery, 612 W. 48th St., Kansas City, MO 64111, 816-753-3647. This is a fun place for kids who want to spoil their beloved pet. The store carries cakes, cookies and other treats just for your favorite dog. Humans can eat them, too!

HOW MANY BILLIONS SERVED?

THE HAPPY MEAL, THAT CHILDREN'S TREAT SERVED AT MCDONALD'S RESTAURANTS AROUND THE WORLD, WAS CREATED RIGHT HERE IN KANSAS CITY. ROBERT BERNSTEIN OF BERNSTEIN-REIN, INC., AN ADVERTISING AGENCY LOCATED ON THE PLAZA, WAS THE ADVERTISING REPRESENTATIVE FOR LOCAL MCDONALD'S IN THE 1970S WHEN HE NOTICED HOW HIS NINE-YEAR-OLD SON WAS ALWAYS READING OR DOING SOMETHING WHILE HE ATE. THE IDEA BERNSTEIN PASSED ON TO HIS DESIGNERS WAS A BOX THAT INCLUDED THE STANDARD BURGER, FRIES AND DRINK, BUT IT HAD TO INCLUDE TEN THINGS KIDS COULD DO WHILE THEY ATE.

IN 1976, THE FIRST HAPPY MEALS WERE SERVED AT MCDONALD'S IN KANSAS CITY, DENVER AND PHOENIX. IN 1979, THE CONCEPT WENT NATIONAL AND IN 1980 BERNSTEIN SOLD THE COPYRIGHT TO MCDONALD'S CORPORATION FOR ONE DOLLAR. IN ALL, BERNSTEIN CREATED 12 HAPPY MEAL BOX THEMES BEFORE SELLING THE RIGHTS. HE HAS THREE OF THOSE ORIGINAL BOXES ON DISPLAY IN HIS OFFICE AS WELL AS A BRONZED HAPPY MEAL BOX PRESENTED TO HIM BY MCDONALD'S FOR HIS INNOVATION.

BERNSTEIN, A KANSAS CITY NATIVE KNOWN FOR HIS COMMUNITY SERVICE, HAS NO IDEA HOW MANY BILLIONS OF HAPPY MEALS HAVE BEEN SERVED SINCE.

Jackson County

South & East of the Plaza

Welcome

Southtown/Brookside/Waldo Association, 6814 Troost, Kansas City, MO 64131, 816-523-5553, www.brooksidekc.org or www.southtown.org.

Assistance

Brookside Mothers Association, www.brooksidemothers.org.

Parents as Teachers, (PAT) 2415 Agnes, Kansas City, MO 64127, 816-418-4860.

Parents as Teacher (PAT), 8111 Oak, Kansas City, MO 64114, 816-418-1761. These are the locations of two of three centers for the Kansas City School District's district-wide program that features private visits with parent-educators as well as group meetings with other parents. There is a toy lending library and resource center. Vision, hearing and physical development evaluation screenings are an important and free part of the program. Parents can take advantage of pre-natal brain development strategies and learning opportunities for their children's development. **Ages: pre-natal to 5.**

Community Centers

Brush Creek Community Center, 3801 Emanuel Cleaver II Blvd., Kansas City, MO 64130, 816-784-4000. The meeting rooms here are filled with programs that include bridge, dominoes, ceramics, karate and arts and crafts. An open gym provides opportunities for volleyball and basketball, and a fitness room provides a great cardiovascular workout. The outdoor pool is open June through September and includes swim lessons.

Hillcrest Community Center, 10401 Hillcrest Rd., Kansas City, MO 64134, 816-784-7000. A wide variety of programs change with the seasons to meet the interests of the community.

Marlborough Community Center, 8200 The Paseo, Kansas City, MO 64131, 816-784-3100. Youth basketball, aerobics, cooking and ceramics are offered in this center that includes a gymnasium and meeting rooms.

Southeast Community Center, 3601 E. 63rd St., Kansas City, MO 64130, 816-784-3200. Peer counseling, tutoring, youth fitness, ceramics and scouting are all offered at this center.

THE GREAT OUTDOORS

Kansas City Missouri Parks and Recreation Department, 4600 E. 63rd St., Kansas City, MO 64130, 816-513-7500, www.kcmo.org. *Because of space limitations, it is impossible to list the wealth of parks, playgrounds, sports activities, and cultural offerings provided by this city department. However, some of the key offerings are listed below:*

Arbor Villa Park, Main St. and 68th Terrace. This triangular shaped park is little more than two acres and has recently been fitted with a sprayground water playground for the kids. The modern playground has rubberized mats and tot swings that are ideal for children two to five years old.

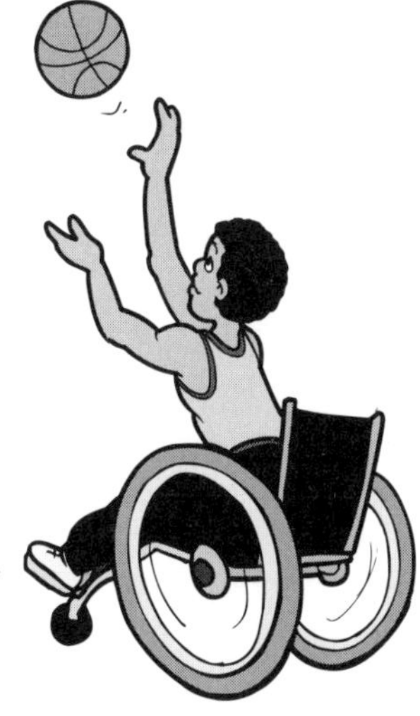

Ashland Square, 23rd St. and Elmwood Ave. The wading pool at this eight-acre park is popular in warm weather, as well as the tennis and basketball courts, the baseball diamond and the modern playground equipment.

Deitrich Park, 27th St. and Gillham Blvd. Although just three acres, this small park has one of the best playgrounds in the city for children with disabilities.

Holmes Park, 70th and Holmes. This 10-acre park has two features unique to the Kansas City Park Department. The first is an outdoor roller hockey rink; the other is a Scout Ring, created as an Eagle Scout project that allows scout groups to build campfires safely. There's also a composite playground with tot swings.

Loose Park, 51st and Wornall. Any time of the year, Jacob Loose Park is filled with families and groups from around the metro enjoying this spectacular 75-acre oasis. Known for its rose garden, huge trees and lake filled with ducks for feeding, Loose Park also has a sprayground, tennis courts, exercise trails and many wide open spaces to spread a blanket and have a family picnic. Loose Park has been named one of the Top 10 Most Beautiful Parks in the country.

Sunnyside Park 82nd and Summit. This 23-acre park is highlighted with a new sprayground, an asphalt exercise trail and three ball diamonds and tennis courts. The playground has rubberized mats and tot swings.

Swope Park, Swope Parkway and Meyer Blvd. As home to the Zoo, Starlight Theatre and numerous activities, the 1800 acres of Swope Park are a mini-nature sanctuary and sports center for urban Kansas City. This is the largest city park in the nation and the top family destination in metropolitan Kansas City. The amenities include two golf courses, a riding academy, a nature center, a frisbee golf course, hiking trails and the city's largest swimming pool that includes a sprayground and sand volleyball court.

Located within Swope Park are:

> **Beanstalk Children's Garden, 6917 Kensington, Kansas City, MO 64132, 816-931-3877**. Families are welcomed to drop in at any time to explore the five different garden areas designed to help children understand how plants grow. School tours available. **Fee. Age: Preschool and up.**

The Kansas City Zoological Park, 6800 Zoo Drive, Kansas City, MO 64132, 816-513-5700, www.kansascityzoo.org. Explore everything from Kenya to the Australian Outback at the 200 acres of the Kansas City Zoo. See elephants trundle down a Botswanian corridor. Stand toe-to-toe with a mob of free-roaming kangaroos. Hand feed a lorikeet from the tropical rainforest. Marvel at one of North America's finest chimpanzee exhibits. Delight at the antics of a newborn eastern black rhinoceros.

In addition to the marvelous animal collection, the Zoo prides itself on outstanding educational opportunities – including overnight safaris – for children, families and classrooms. For specific educational programs, such as the Nocturnal Safaris and Zoo School, call 816-513-5723.

Lake of the Woods Riding Stables, 7303 Oakwood, Kansas City, MO 64132, 816-513-4638. Learn English, western or trail riding at these stables in Swope Park. Private and group lessons available. **Fee. Ages: 5 and up.**

Lakeside Nature Center, 4701 E. Gregory Blvd., Kansas City, MO 64132, 816-513-8960, www.lakesidenaturecenter.org. This center on ten acres in Swope Park is a wildlife rehabilitation program for Missouri native wildlife. The center has year-round classes for children and parents that include tours of the center, bird walks, wildflower classes, fossil walks and nature hikes. Summer of Science Camp is perfect for the young naturalist 6-12 years old. Parents and older children can also be a part of the center's volunteer activities that include the care and feeding of injured animals, such as bald eagles and bobcats. **Ages: Preschool and up.**

Starlight Theatre, 816-333-9481. A summer performance at Starlight, the nation's largest outdoor theatre, is a Kansas City tradition for many families. For an extra treat, plan on a backstage tour that includes dressing rooms, props, the orchestra pit and a chance to appear on stage for a minute without an audience. There is no charge for the tours that begin at 6 p.m. before an 8:30 p.m. curtain. **Ages: 6 and up.**

Summer Camps

Barstow Summer Program, 11511 State Line Rd., Kansas City, MO 64114, 816-942-3255, www.barstowschool.org. More than 250 classes keep kids of all ages busy in the summer months. These range from academic enrichment to sports to adventure learning. **Ages: preschool to 12th grade.**

Pembroke Day School Summer Camp, 400 W. 51st St., or 5121 State Line Rd., Kansas City, MO 64112, 816-753-1300, www.pembrokehill.org. The modestly priced day sessions occupy kids with painting, swimming, drama, archery, puppet-making, field trips and more. **Ages: pre-school to 12th grade.**

Notre Dame de Sion, 3823 Locust, Kansas City, MO 64109, 816 753-3810 (elementary) or **10631 Wornall Rd., Kansas City, MO 64114, 816-942-3282** (high school), www.ndsion.edu.

Things to Do

Alexander Majors Home, 8201 State Line Rd., Kansas City, MO, 816-333-5556. Majors, whose freighting firms paved the way west, built his farmhouse in 1856 as the earliest headquarters of the Pony Express. The home is open for tours most afternoons and a barn is available for rental. **Fee. Ages: 2nd to 6th grade.**

Benjamin Ranch, 6401 E. 87th St., Kansas City, MO 64138, 816-761-5055, www.benjaminranch.com. Here's a taste of the country for kids of all ages. In summer, hayrides are available; winter brings sleigh rides and indoor pony parties. There's a party barn, shelter house for picnics and an annual rodeo. **Fee. Ages: 5 and up.**

Black Archives of Mid-America, 2033 Vine St., Kansas City, MO 64108, 816-483-1300. This center holds one of the country's most complete collections of paintings and sculptures by black artists. There is information about black musicians, writers, and local black leaders. Exhibits trace the history of blacks in Kansas City. **Free. Ages: 8 and up.**

Board of Trade, 4800 Main, Kansas City, MO 64112, 816-753-7500, www.kcbt.com. One of the country's largest commodities and futures exchanges, the Board of Trade provides weekly tours that feature a glimpse of the bustling activities on the trading room floor. **Free. Ages: High School.**

Bruce R. Watkins Cultural Heritage Center, 3700 Blue Parkway, Kansas City, MO 64130, 816-784-4444. This center honors the contributions of African-American residents to Kansas City's history with rotating exhibits, hands-on displays and stage performances. A Hall of Fame includes oral histories told by many of Kansas City's legendary African-American leaders.
Free. **Ages: 8 and up.**

Freedom Fountain. Adjacent to the Bruce R. Watkins Center, this fountain incorporates the image of Kansas City jazz and honors the men and women who first came to Kansas City as slaves.

Cleveland Chiropractic College, 6401 Rockhill Rd., Kansas City, MO 64131, 816-501-0100, www.cleveland.edu. It sounds sort of gross, but if your children are interested in medical or forensic science careers, the college offers tours of its cadaver lab. **Ages: High School only.**

Communiversity, 5327 Holmes, Kansas City, MO 64110, 816-235-1448, www.umkc.edu/commu. Communiversity introduces you and your kids to a world of people and ideas through classes, events and services unique to this area. Offerings for kids include arts and craft classes, calligraphy, cartooning and horseback riding. **Fee. Ages: 5 and up.**

TRIVIA

BRUCE R. WATKINS WAS KANSAS CITY'S FIRST AFRICAN-AMERICAN TO SERVE ON THE CITY COUNCIL AND MAKE A SERIOUS RUN FOR MAJOR. AS A CITY COUNCILMAN, HE SUCCESSFULLY FOUGHT FOR CIVIL RIGHTS ISSUES IN THE CITY. A MAJOR IMPROVEMENT TO HIGHWAY 71, WHICH OPENED IN NOVEMBER 2001, IS NAMED IN HIS HONOR AND LINKS MUCH OF SOUTHERN JACKSON COUNTY TO DOWNTOWN AND THE URBAN CORE.

Golf Discount, 1 E. 135th St., Kansas City, MO 64145, 816-941-9000. A wonderful 18-hole mini-golf course keeps the young ones entertained while older children can practice their swing on the driving range or take golf lessons. The center is open year-round. **Fee. Ages: All.**

John Wornall House, 6115 Wornall Rd., Kansas City, MO 64113, 816-444-1858, www.wornallhouse.org. This 1858 home was used as a field hospital during the Civil War's Battle of Westport. A tour provides insights into the lives of Missouri settlers. Check out activities for children such as the Christmas Holiday Class or the Summer Pioneer Camp. A special patch is available for Girl Scout troops. Educational trunks are available for loan to schools. **Fee. Ages: 8 and up.**

Kansas City Clay Guild, 200 W. 74th St., Kansas City, MO 64114, 816-363-1373. Kids can make their own pottery by hand or on a pottery wheel during Saturday morning classes, or families can come together on Friday and Saturday night for fun classes. Summer classes offer more intense creative opportunities. **Fee. Ages: 6 to 12.**

Kansas City Young Audiences, 5601 Wyandotte, Kansas City, MO 64113, 816-531-4022, www.kcya.org. Bring your children here to stir their creative spirits. Located behind St. Therese Academy, Kansas City Young Audiences offers after-school, weekend and summer classes in music, dance, drama, creative writing, and the visual arts. This organization is the largest arts education provider in the Midwest, providing more than 2,000 workshops a year. **Ages: 5 and up. Fee.**

KSHB TV, 4720 Oak St., Kansas City, MO 64112, 816,753-4141, www.nbcactionnews.com. Learn about the weather with NBC Action News Chief Meteorologist, Gary Lezak, and his dogs Windy and Stormy. Lezak's visits to schools are both educational and entertaining. Just send a formal request to the station to the attention of the Publicity Coordinator. Then wait to see your school on TV! **Free. Ages: Kindergarten and up.**

Mac and Seitz Old Ballgame, 13705 Holmes Rd., Kansas City, MO 64145, 816-942-9992. Owned by Royals legends Mike McFarland and Kevin Seitzer, this huge facility has a number of indoor batting cages and hitting tunnels, as well as a full-size indoor infield. There's a weight room and track and two outdoor fields. Coaching is available for hitting, pitching, fielding and catching. **Ages: 5 and up. Fee.**

New Explorers Program, 816-234-5520, www.kcpd.org. For young adults living in the Metro Patrol Division, the Kansas City Police Department sponsors this program that provides practical experience in law enforcement careers. **Ages: 14 to 18.**

Russell Stover Candies, 320 E. 51st St., Kansas City, MO 64111, 816-753-1677, www.russellstover.com. Tours of the Kansas City original are tailored to the age and interests of the group, but all tours include samples of the candies. Tours by appointment. **Fee. Ages: All.**

Satchel Paige Stadium, Swope Parkway and 47th St., Kansas City, MO 64130, 816-513-7500. Named in honor of the legendary pitcher for the Kansas City A's, this 2,000-seat stadium hosts several inner-city league teams while honoring those who played in the Negro Leagues. Stop by and enjoy a game some afternoon.

Toy and Miniature Museum, 5235 Oak St., Kansas City, MO 64110, 816-333-2055, http://www.umkc.edu/tmm. Young and old alike enjoy this fascinating collection of antique toys, exact-scale miniature doll houses and furnishing, and a large-scale working train. The museum also has one of the world's largest collections of marbles. Storytellers perform every Saturday. **Fee. Ages: preschool and up.**

UMKC Geosciences Museum, Flarsheim Science and Technology Building, #271, 5110 Rock Hill Rd., Kansas City, MO 64110, 816-235-1334. The museum displays a variety of unusual rocks and minerals, plus gemstones, fossils, petrified wood and a "sea lily." Kids really like the set of rocks with water bubbles stuck inside. Guided tours by appointment. **Free. Ages: Kindergarten and up.**

FUN FOOD

Foo's Fabulous Frozen Custard, 6235 Brookside Plaza, Kansas City, MO 64131, 816-523-2520. The numbers of flavors are endless here because you can choose any combination and flavor you like and watch while they make it. Kids like the abundance of sprinkles placed on the orders. Adults appreciate the personal service that makes any stop in Brookside a treat in itself.

McLain's Bakery, 7422 Wornall Rd., Kansas City, MO 64114, 816-523-9911. Since 1945, Kansas City birthday cakes have come from this family-owned business. In addition to the McLain's signature "chocolate cup cookie," a pecan swirl sort of thing with icing on top, the bakery has great muffins, Danish, coffee cakes and other cookies.

Pickerman's Soup and Sandwiches, 116 W. 63rd St., Kansas City, MO 64131, 816-444-6444. Kids can get a great peanut butter and jelly sandwich, but the variety of 12 homemade cookies, fresh out of the oven, is a draw for people of all ages.

SPECIAL SHOPS

Brookside Toy and Science, 330 W. 63rd St., Kansas City, MO 64131, 816-523-4501. This long time Brookside shop sells toys, dolls and science kits and equipment, telescopes and more.

Dime Store, 314 W. 63rd St., Kansas City, MO 64131, 816-444-7207. Today's kids know malls, but have a great time in this traditional dime store, which has been serving Brookside families for more than 60 years. It has a wooden floor and lots of interesting things to look at.

Reading Reptile, 328 W. 63rd St., Kansas City, MO 64131, 816-753-0441, www.readingreptile.com. The metropolitan area's premiere children's bookstore offers numerous special events to encourage the reading habits of young people. These include writing contests, storytellers, author's appearances and more. Some are free and some are fee-based.

National Poison Prevention Week

IS ALWAYS THE THIRD WEEK IN MARCH.

"CHILDREN ACT FAST—
SO DO POISONS!"

FOR MORE INFORMATION ON HOW TO PREVENT CHILDHOOD POISONINGS, VISIT WWW.POISONPREVENTION.ORG.

EASTERN JACKSON COUNTY AND CASS COUNTY

INCLUDES BLUE SPRINGS, INDEPENDENCE, SUGAR CREEK, RAYTOWN, GRANDVIEW, LEE'S SUMMIT AND BELTON

WELCOME

Missouri Welcome Center, I-70 at the Truman Sports Complex, 816-889-3330. Stop here for tons of information on places to go and things to do on the Missouri side of metropolitan Kansas City. Lots of discount coupons are available, as well as maps to some of these hidden destinations.

BLUE SPRINGS, INDEPENDENCE, SUGAR CREEK

WELCOME

City of Independence, Division of Tourism, 111 E. Maple St., Independence, MO 64050, 816-325-7111, www.independencemo.com.

Independence Chamber of Commerce, 210 W. Truman Rd., Independence, MO 64050, 816-252-4745, www.independencechamber.com.

Blue Springs Chamber of Commerce, 1000 S.W. Main St., Blue Springs, MO 64015, 816-229-8558, www.bluespringschamber.com.

COMMUNITY CENTERS

Blue Springs Civic Center, 2000 W. Ashton Dr., Blue Springs, MO 64015, 816-224-1300. Meeting and conference facilities here can accommodate up to 300 people and the auditorium seats more than 700. Fun programs for the whole family are offered here year-round.

Sermon Center/Toddler Town, 201 N. Dodgion, Independence, MO 64050, 816-325-7370. A gymnasium, game room and weight room are always available for community use, but every Monday, Wednesday and Friday mornings from October through March, the gymnasium is reconstructed into Toddler Town, an indoor play village for kids 1 through 5. Gymnastics for children 3 through 15 are offered in the summer.

THE GREAT OUTDOORS

Blue Springs Parks and Recreation, 903 W. Main, Blue Springs, MO 64015, 816-228-0137, www.bluespringsgov.com**.** Ask about *Picnic Kits* – a wide variety of recreation equipment available for rent for your family or group outing.

Independence Parks and Recreation, 201 Dodgion, Independence, MO 64050, 816-325-7360.

Jackson County Parks and Recreation, 22807 Woods Chapel Rd., Blue Springs, MO 64015, 816-795-8200, www.jacksongov.org**.** One of the oldest and largest county park systems in the United States, then Presiding Judge Harry S Truman created this system in 1927 that today totals more than 22,000 acres. It includes outstanding summer day camp offerings and the most comprehensive program in the metropolitan area for children with disabilities.

PASSIVE ACTIVITIES, SUCH AS WATCHING TV, DEPRIVE A CHILD'S BRAIN OF SENSORY, HANDS-ON ACTIVITIES THAT SIMULATE BRAIN GROWTH.

SOURCE: WWW.KCBRAINCHILD.ORG

Special Area Parks and Playgrounds

Baumgardner Park, 2401 N.W. Ashton Dr., Blue Springs, MO 64015, 816-228-0188 – pool only. This 12-acre park has it all! First, it's home to the Centennial Pool-Plex *(see page 78)* that includes indoor and outdoor swimming, waterslides and sprayers. The park also has sand volleyball, tennis courts, and playgrounds with tot swings.

Burr Oak Woods Conservation Nature Center, 1401 N.W. Park Rd., Blue Springs, MO 64015, 816-228-3766. More than 1,100 acres of exhibits, wildlife habitat and discovery trails make up this urban forest and wildlife refuge. Children love the exhibits that feature deer, snakes, frogs, ducks and a bald eagle. There's a huge aquarium stocked with native fish and an outdoor bird feeding area where youngsters can view the creatures in their natural environment. The center offers an impressive number of fun and educational classes and activities for those of all ages.

Burris Old Mill Park, 112 N.W. Woods Chapel Rd., Blue Springs, MO. This 14-acre park is where the city of Blue Springs was founded and is the site of the city's first skateboard park, a 7,500 square foot skating facility added in the fall of 2004. Skaters enjoy 22 obstacles ranging from half-pipes to a pyramid. There's also a walking trail, ball fields and a playground.

Burrough's Audubon Center and Library, 21509 S.W. Woods Chapel Rd., Blue Springs, MO 64105, 816-795-8177. Children learn about nature at this center that contains exhibits of birds' nests, insects and butterflies. More than 20 outdoor bird feeders attract a variety of birds to watch each day. The children's library contains more than 2,500 age-appropriate books and videos about birds.

An adult's vocabulary is largely determined by the words heard during the first five years of life. Talking to your baby helps the brain grow! Source: www.kcbrainchild.org.

Fleming Park, 1 mile east of Hwy. 291 and Woods Chapel Rd., Blue Springs, 816-795-8200. This is the largest of the Jackson County parks, covering more than 7,800 acres with nearly 1,000 acres of lake water for boating, fishing and sailing. Kids love feeding the fish at the two full-service marinas. Nearly every outdoor sport and educational activity imaginable is available at Fleming Park, including: sail, motor and pontoon boat rentals; polo fields, radio controlled airplane fields; archery, ten hiking trails; sand beaches with shower and restroom facilities; soccer, football, softball and all-purpose fields; and numerous recreation facilities. Also included are:

> **Kemper Outdoor Education Center, 816-229-8980**. Woodlands, wetlands, garden ponds, butterfly gardens and an arboretum are available for your exploration, as well as an endless number of educational and environmental programs.
>
> **Native Hoofed Animal Enclosure, 816-229-8980**. A Jeep ride through this 100-acre enclosure gets you and the kids up close and personal with buffalo, elk and other animals of the wild that once roamed this area freely. Families may view the animals at any time, but Jeep rides are for groups of 12 or more only. **Fee.**
>
> **Missouri Town 1855, 816-524-8770.** This reconstructed 1850s farming community is comprised of more than 30 original structures that make up a charming village. Children love the opportunity to see barnyard animals, such as free-running chickens, sheep and horses. The volunteer staff, dressed in period clothing, tells stories while demonstrating chores done by frontier Americans. **Ages: 1st grade and up. Free.**

George Owens Nature Park, 1601 S. Speck Rd., Independence, MO 64057, 816-325-7115. This park has two fishing lakes, four miles of walking trails and a nature center with an outdoor habitat filled with all sorts of critters. The park also has a primitive campground with restrooms. A full-time naturalist coordinates numerous educational programs.

McCoy Park, Hwy. 24, Independence, MO. While visiting the Harry S. Truman Presidential Library, make plans to have a picnic lunch or enjoy a few minutes of outdoor activity at this nearby 17-acre park that includes a sprayground added in 2005, a modern playground, horseshoe pits and a paved walking trail.

Pink Hill Park, 2715 N.W. Park Rd., Blue Springs, MO. This 40 acres adjacent to Burr Oak Woods Nature Center has a BMX race track, five shelter houses, a handicapped-accessible playground with tot swings, horseshoes, sand volleyball and tennis, and a walking/jogging path.

Rotary Park at Railroad Lake, S. Hwy. 7 and Vesper St., Blue Springs, MO. Centering around a railroad theme, kids will love the walking trails, fishing lake and modern playgrounds with tot swings. Tennis courts are also available. The festive gazebo is used for numerous special events, including Sunday night concerts in the summer.

THINGS TO DO

B&D Skate Center, 36th and Noland Ct., Independence, MO 64055, 816-252-1084. For more than 25 years, this roller rink has been available for private parties, school events and family outings. **Ages: All. Fee.**

Bingham-Waggoner Estate, 313 W. Pacific, Independence, MO, 64050, 816-461-3491 or 325-7111, www.bwestate.org**.** Built in 1855, this private home eventually became the residence of Missouri artist George Caleb Bingham. In 1879, the home was purchased by Peter and William Waggoner, who expanded the home to 26 rooms. Kids will love the room filled with more than $5,000 worth of antique toys and the hide-and-seek crawl spaces on the third floor. **Ages: Kindergarten and up. Fee.**

Centennial Pool-Plex, 2401 Ashton Drive, Blue Springs, MO 64015, 816-228-0188, www.ci.blue-springs.mo.us**.** This public swimming facility includes 25-yard, 50-meter and kiddie pools. Lessons and classes are offered throughout the year. A major advantage – it's 82-degrees year-round inside and not too crowded in the cooler weather months. **Ages: All. Fee.**

Central Jackson County Fire Protection District, 805 N.E. Jefferson, Blue Springs, MO 64014, 816-229-2522, www.cjcfpd.org. Kids get to turn on the lights and sirens of a firetruck as a part of this popular tour of the firehouse and administrative offices. The safety presentation gives youngsters an idea of how firefighters work under pressure. There's also a visit from a "fire monster," who is really a firefighter in a bunker suit. Tours need to be scheduled two weeks in advance. **Ages: Preschool and up. Free.**

Children's Peace Pavilion, 1001 W. Walnut, Independence, MO 64050, 816-833-1000, ext. 1357. www.cofchrist.org **or** www.kidpeace.org. This is the only children's peace museum of its kind in the country and explores the concept of peace for individuals, humanity and the planet in a number of hands-on interactive exhibits that encourages kids to think about how best to achieve peace. Through coloring, puppet shows and any number of activities, kids of all faiths learn the meaning and pathway to peace. The Peace Pavilion is a part of the World Headquarters of the Community of Christ Church. **Ages: All. Free.**

Cool Crest Family Fun Center, 10735 East U.S. 40, Independence, MO 64055, 816-358-0088, www.coolcrest.com. Located one mile east of the Truman Sports Complex, this family-owned operation has entertained Kansas City kids since the 1950s. Included are miniature golf, a game room with pinball and video games, go-carts, a batting cage and a great pizzeria. Cool Crest is incredibly cool for birthday parties. **Ages: All. Fee.**

Dillingham-Lewis Home, 15th and Main, Blue Springs, MO 64015, 816-224-4910. This early 20th century pioneer home holds tours by appointment and offers several special events during the year. Kids are fascinated by the old furnace vents, ice cream freezer and ice box, Victrola, pump, and other artifacts on the premises. **Ages: 7 and up. Free.**

Englewood Theatre, 10917 Winner Rd., Independence, MO 64052, 816-252-2463, www.englewoodplaza.com. Take your kids to see the movie classics in the setting they were meant to be seen in – a 1949 art-deco theatre with a 50-foot screen. Current movies are also shown here. Special live performances are also held here, so check regularly for current events. **Ages: Vary. Fee.**

1859 Marshal's Home and Jail Museum, 217 N. Main St., Independence, MO 64050, 816-252-1892, www.jchs.org**.** Four buildings comprise this museum, which got a major make-over in 2004. Children seem to like the jail cells, especially when they learn that Frank James was held here, as well as another prisoner who was nine years old. Included are an old school house and the marshal's residence. This is a good visit for those children studying Missouri history and the Civil War. **Ages: 4th grade and up. Fee.**

Family Golf Park, 1501 N.E. U.S. 40, Blue Springs, MO 64015, 816-228-1550, www.familygolfpark.com**.** Bumper boats, 9-hole par 3 golf course and driving range, two 18-hole miniature golf courses, a kid's pro shop and game room make this a great destination for birthday parties, rainy days or any family outing. Kids under 40 inches tall play free on the miniature golf courses. **Ages: All. Fee.**

Fort Osage National Historic Site, 105 Osage St., Sibley, MO 64088, 816-650-5737, www.historicfortosage.com. Built in 1808 by William Clark of Lewis and Clark fame, this first U.S. outpost in the Louisiana Purchase has lots of frontier buildings to explore as well as Osage Indian artifacts and exhibits reflecting the area's early history. Drive 14 miles northeast of Independence and take U.S. 24 east to Buckner. Turn north on Sibley Street and follow the signs. **Ages: All. Fee.**

I-70 Drive-In, 8791 E. 40 Highway, Kansas City, MO 64129, 816-861-0500. Family-style tailgating begins an hour before dusk at the four screens of the I-70, where kids 11 and under get in free. The drive-in is open all year long. **Ages: All. Fee.**

IBEX Climbing Gym, 801 S. Outer Road, Blue Springs, MO 64015, 816-228-9988, www.climbibex.com**.** Ropes, rocks and boulders along this 32-foot wall with vertical and overhang elements contribute to the fun and challenge of the 6,800 square foot center. Kids of all ages can climb but you must have a waiver signed by a legal guardian and notarized if you are under 18. **Ages: 5 and up. Fee.**

Independence Center Carousel, Independence Center Mall, Hwy. 291 and I-70, Independence, MO 64050, 816-795-8600. Built in Venice, Italy, this double-decker carousel holds up to 70 riders on a fun, five-minute ride. An adjacent playground includes bigger-than-life hamburgers for kids to play on. **Ages: All. Free.**

***The Independence Examiner*, 410 S. Liberty, Independence, MO 64050, 816-254-8600, ext. 129, www.examiner.net.** This newspaper publishes daily news for Independence and Blue Springs. The tour explains the operation and children get to see how reporters work, how ads are designed and how the presses run. Two weeks notice for tours is necessary. **Ages: 3rd grade and up. Free.**

Independence Farmer's Market, Truman Rd. between Main and Liberty, 816-650-3233. Farmers from around the area sell their produce on Wednesday and Saturday mornings from May through September. Children used to eating canned and frozen produce get a chance to taste fresh-from-the-ground veggies. **Ages: All.**

Independence Police Department, 223 N. Memorial Dr., Independence, MO 64050, 816-325-7317, www.independencemo.org. Kids get to tour the detective bureau, radio and squad rooms. They'll learn about the law and how to obey it, plus they'll get plenty of safety tips. Allow about 45 minutes for the tour. **Ages: 5 and up. Free.**

Kansas City International Raceway, 8201 Noland Rd., Kansas City, MO 64138, 816-358-6700, www.kcir.net. On Wednesday and Friday nights, those 16 and older can drive their own cars on the track. Other evenings, drag racing, street stocks, high performance and funny cars provide entertainment for those of all ages. Kids eight and older can build their own race car in the Junior Dragster program. Smaller children may be bothered by the loud noises. **Ages: All. Fee.**

Lunar Bowl, 2001 N.W. 7 Hwy., Blue Springs, MO 64014, 816-220-7722, www.lunarbowl.com. They say it's like no place on Earth, certainly not in Kansas City, with 32 lanes of galactic bowling, incredible sound and lighting and a great arcade. This is a birthday party dream and parents can get away, without getting away, for a few moments in the Blue Moon Lounge. **Ages: All. Fee.**

Mid-Continent Public Library Genealogy & Local History Branch, 317 U.S. Hwy. 24, Independence, MO 64050, 816-252-7228, www.mcpl.lib.mo.us**.** At this library branch, you can print the front page of area newspapers for the day you were born. A TeenGenes group, ages 13 to 19, explores family history. **Ages: All. Free.**

National Frontier Trails Center, 318 W. Pacific Ave., Independence, MO 64050, 816-325-7575, www.frontiertrailscenter.com**.** This is the only interpretive center in the nation devoted to the Santa Fe, Oregon and California trails, which opened the American West to white exploration and settlement. Even kids will sit through the award-winning introductory film that prepares them for their trip through the museum's many exhibits. **Ages: 2nd grade and up. Fee.**

Puppetry Arts Institute, 11025 E. Winner Rd., Independence, MO 64052, 816-833-9777, www.hazelle.org**.** Kids get to make their own puppets and then put on a puppet show in this wonderfully creative center that honors Hazelle Rollins, a world-renowned name in puppeteering. In addition, children will enjoy a tour of marionettes from around the world, and the many puppet shows presented by professional puppeteers. This is a great place for birthday parties. **Ages: 5 and up. Fee.**

Sibley Orchard, 4121 California Ave., Sibley, MO 64088, 816-650-5535. Starting in mid-summer, come here for U-Pick blackberries, followed by other fruits and vegetables in season. The autumn months bring hayrides through the pumpkin patch. **Ages: All.**

South Noland Road Driving Range, 7601 S. Noland Rd., Kansas City, MO 64138, 816-353-3229. If your kids are old enough to stand and can hold a golf club, they can begin lessons here with private golf instructors. Open year-round when the temperature is 40 degrees or above. **Ages: All. Fee.**

Sports City, 425 N.E. Mock Avenue, Blue Springs, MO 64014, 816-229-1314, www.sportscitykc.com**.** This 76,000 sq. ft. indoor facility features two full size arena soccer fields, a gymnasium for basketball and volleyball, four batting cages, Lazer tag, an arcade and a casual restaurant for teams and families to enjoy after the game. A Little Kickers soccer program is open for kids beginning at 18 months. **Ages: All. Fee.**

Stephenson's Orchard, 6700 Lee's Summit Rd., Kansas City, MO 64136, 816-373-5138, www.stephensons.bigstep.com**.** This is the place to come during apple or strawberry-picking time. Fall tours of the orchard, packing house and cider mill are available to schools and organized groups by reservation. The kids will need to walk on this tour, but even the smallest child can reach the branches for apples and berries. **Ages: 4 and up. Fee.**

Sterling Bowl, 11216 E. U.S. 24, Sugar Creek, MO 64052, 816-252-2111. This center offers a Friday night family "rock-n-bowl" and a junior league on Saturday afternoons. Kids enrolled in the "Have A Ball" program receive a free bowling ball to keep at the end of a league season. **Ages: 6 and up. Fee**.

Twin Drive-In, 291 and Kentucky Rd., Kansas City, MO 64056, 816-257-2234. Kids love the playground and atmosphere at this drive-in that has been welcoming families for more than 35 years. Parents love that kids under 11 get in free. Open approximately April 1 through November 1. **Ages: All. Fee.**

Watson's Family Fun and Skate Center, 513 Keystone Dr., Blue Springs, MO 64015, 816-229-7793. This rink with a wooden floor has organized family nights suitable for all skills and ages. It's also available for private parties. **Ages: All. Fee**.

Vaile Mansion-DeWitt Museum, 1500 N. Liberty St., Independence, MO 64050, 816-325-7111. One of the best examples of Victorian architecture in the United States, this 1882 mansion has a second floor room the kids especially love. The woodwork is painted with dozens of little faces and animals. Open April through October and Thanksgiving through the end of December. **Ages: 6 and up. Fee.**

HARRY'S HOMETOWN

Much of the history of Harry S Truman and these sites can be found at www.nps.gove/hstr. A walking tour brochure of the area is available from the City of Independence Tourism at 111 E. Maple St. Independence, MO 64050, 816-325-7111, www.independencemo.com.

Harry S Truman Library, U.S. 24 and Delaware St., 816-833-1400, www.trumanlibrary.org. An extraordinary Thomas Hart Benton mural greets you as you walk through the door. Kids may particularly like the Oval office exhibit and automobiles owned by the president and his family. Throughout the exhibit, activities challenge young people to put themselves in Harry Truman's shoes. Activities include trying on period clothing, sorting mail, writing letters and making campaign buttons. Teachers should ask about the White House Decision Center and the Truman Footlocker project. **Ages: All. Fee.**

Harry S Truman Railroad Station, Grand and Pacific. This depot, which figured in Truman's 1948 Whistle Stop campaign, is a stop for daily Amtrak service into Kansas City. Take kids on a quick round-trip while talking about presidential history.

Truman Home, 219 N. Delaware St., 816-254-2720. This is where Harry and Bess lived for more than 50 years. Tours include a 12-minute slide show at the visitor center and a 15-minute tour of the residence. You must reserve your tickets in person on a first-come, first-served basis on the day of the tour at the Harry S Truman National Historic Site Visitor Center, 223 N. Main, which is in downtown Independence. Kids may get a Jr. Ranger badge for completing a workbook about the site. Those **under 16 get in free.**

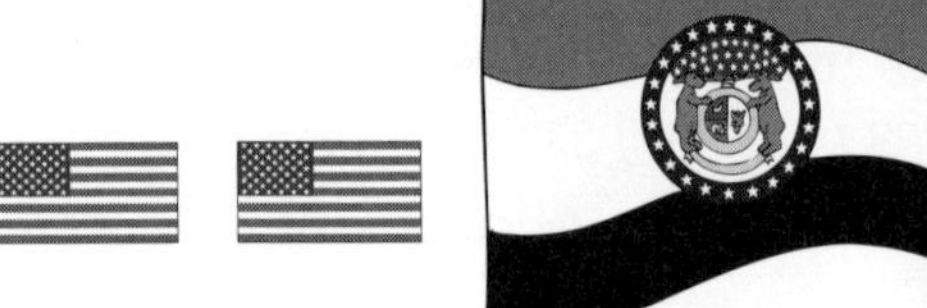

Harry S Truman Courtroom and Office, Main and Maple St., 816-252-7454. This is where our 33rd president began the political career that led him to the White House. You'll see Judge Truman's restored quarters and an audiovisual presentation about his life and courtship with Bess. The courtroom is open Monday through Friday. **Ages: All. Fee.**

1827 Log Courthouse, 107 W. Kansas Ave., 816-325-7111. The first courthouse in Jackson County, this is also the oldest structure open to the public in Independence. During the 1920s and 30s, the building housed the Community Welfare league, of which Bess Truman was vice-chair. Judge Harry Truman held court here in 1932 as the main courthouse was being remodeled.

Also plan to visit the Truman Farm Home in Grandview (page 94).

An alert reader may have noted that no period appears after the S in Harry S Truman's name. We have not made a typographical or proofreading error. The late president did not have a middle name, just the letter S, after which he never placed a period, so neither did we.

Fun Food and Treats

Courthouse Exchange Restaurant, 113 W. Lexington Ave., Independence, MO 64050, 816-252-0344. This place serves breakfast all day and has some of the best cinnamon rolls you've ever tasted.

Clinton's Old Fashioned Soda Fountain and Gift Shop, 100 W. Maple, Independence, MO 64050, 816-833-2046. This is where Harry Truman held his first job. At age 14, he made $3 a week sweeping floors and making soda fountain treats. The shop has been restored to the look of when Harry worked here.

Stephenson's Apple Farm Restaurant, 16401 E. 40 Highway, Kansas City, MO 64136, 816-373-5400, www.stephenson's.bigstep.com**.** This family restaurant is famous for its hickory-smoked chicken, ham and pork chops, apple cider and luscious apple dumplings. You might want to call for reservations for Sunday brunch. Child-sized servings are available.

SPECIAL SHOPS

Apple Tree Bookstore, 204 W. Maple St., Independence, MO 64050, 816-833-7600, www.appletreebookstore.com**.** This gaily-decorated store is owned by a former elementary school librarian who gives a free bookmark with every purchase. Mother Goose visits every Saturday and the back room is available for birthday parties, tea parties and scrapbooking parties.

Belton, Raytown, Grandview, Lee's Summit

Welcome

Belton Chamber of Commerce, 512 Main St., Belton, MO 64012, 816-331-2420, www.beltonmochamber.com.

Raytown Chamber of Commerce, 5909 Raytown Trfwy., Raytown, MO 64133, 816-353-8500, www.raytownchamber.com

Grandview Chamber of Commerce, Bank Midwest Building, 12500 S. U.S. 71 Hwy., Grandview, MO 64030, 816-761-6505, www.grandview.org

Lee's Summit Chamber of Commerce, 220 S.E. Main St., Lee's Summit, MO 64063, 816-524-2424, www.lschamber.com.

Assistance

Parents As Teachers, 1151 N.E. Colbern Rd., Lee's Summit, MO 64086, 816-986-3360.

Giant Step, 244 N.E. Chipman Rd., Lee's Summit, MO, 64063, 816-524-1234, www.giantstep.com**.** This day care provider specializes in children with disabilities and their siblings.

Grandview Mom's Club, P.O. Box 704, Belton, MO 64012, 816-331-8782.

The Learnables Foreign Language Courses, 12220 Blue Ridge Blvd., Grandview, MO 64030, 816-765-8855, www.learnables.com**.** This local company offers language programs in Spanish, French, German, Russian, Hebrew, Japanese, Chinese and Czech for children beginning at age seven.

COMMUNITY CENTERS

Lee's Summit Recreation Center, 110 SW Blue Parkway, Lee's Summit, MO 64063, 816-969-7780. Indoor basketball and volleyball courts are the primary features of this center located in Harris Memorial Park.

Legacy Park Community Center, 901 N.E. Blackwell Parkway, Lee's Summit, MO 64086, 816-969-7529. This new facility has two indoor pools, one lap and the other leisure with slides and spray features. There's also a gym, racquetball courts and a fitness center.

The View, 13500 Byars Rd., Grandview, MO 64030, 816-316-4888. Located in Meadowmere Park, this new facility for the city of Grandview features a fabulous swimming facility, with lap pool and a zero depth entry pool with a water slide and lazy river. There are also two gyms, a rock climbing wall and a fitness center.

THE GREAT OUTDOORS

Grandview Parks and Recreation, 13500 Byars Rd., Grandview, MO 64030, 816-316-4879, www.gvview.org.

Lee's Summit Parks and Recreation, 307 S.W. Market, Lee's Summit, MO 64063, 816-969-7494, www.lees-summit.mo.us. The city offers summer camps for 5 to 11 year-olds, and is one of the few in the metro area that offers a separate full-day summer camp for 12 to 14-year-olds.

Raytown Parks and Recreation, 5912 Lane, Raytown, MO 64133, 816-358-4100, www.raytownparks.com. The city runs tennis leagues and volleyball for youth and a Fishing Derby in September for Raytown kids under 15.

SPECIAL AREA PARKS AND PLAYGROUNDS

Harris Memorial Park, Jefferson St. and Blue Pkwy, Lee's Summit. Children especially love Safety Town where they can ride their vehicles in the pretend town with stop signs, storefronts and street lines painted on the asphalt. This 23-acre park also has an outdoor pool (816-969-7499), eight horseshoe pits, a climbing rock and a playground shaped like a castle.

Howard Park, 3498 N.E. Independence, Lee's Summit. An in-line skating rink for roller hockey and a skate park attracts kids to this 23-acre park that also has a one mile paved hiking trail and a playground shaped like a boat.

Longview Lake Park, I-470 S. between Lee's Summit and Grandview, 816-966-0131. Once a part of the Longview Farm, this 4,800-acre park features a model airfield for radio controlled aircraft, bike paths, boating, golfing, swimming, hiking and horseback riding. The swimming beach has a large area of shallow water where kids can splash. Two handicapped accessible fishing docks complement numerous fishing facilities. Camping and ballooning contribute to the attractions that bring more than one million people a year to this park.

James A. Reed Memorial Wildlife Area, 13101 S.E. Ranson Rd., Lee's Summit, MO 64082, 816-622-0900. This Missouri Conservation Department area has fishing lakes and nature trails that are abundant with songbirds, deer, migrating water fowl and wildlife. There are fishing clinics for kids 12 and younger at the children's pond, which is well-stocked for a guaranteed catch. **Ages: All.**

Henry C. Kritser Park, 75th and Woodson, Raytown. Named after a pioneer to the area, this 11-acre park, dedicated in 2001, has two age-specific playgrounds that are handicapped accessible and have tot swings. There are also baseball and soccer fields here, as well as an .8 mile walking path and modern restrooms.

Meadowmere Park, 13610 Byars Rd., 1 mile east of Hwy 71, Grandview. This park has something for everyone, including a baby pool with geyser, a handicapped-accessible playground with tot swings and spring animals. A skateboard park was added in 2004. One playground is in the shape of a castle. There are also sand volleyball courts, a paved walking trail that connects to the Longview trail, plus numerous soccer and football fields.

Powell Gardens, 20 miles east of Lee's Summit on U.S. 50, 816-697-2600, www.powellgardens.org. Powell Gardens is 915-acre botanical garden with educational and entertaining programs for people of all ages all year long. It's also a great place just to go for a nice, quiet walk. Special kids' programs focus on insects and the environment. There's a great café and gift shop as well. **Ages: All. Fee.**

Upper Banner Park, 520 N.E. Noleen Rd., Lee's Summit. This 14-acre park has a number of ramps loved by skateboarders as well as tennis courts and a modern playground.

THINGS TO DO

Aaron's Family Fun Center, 17070 Aaron's Lane, Belton, MO 64102, 816-322-0488, www.aaronsfamilyfuncenter.com. Fun is indeed the word at the center that includes 32 lanes of bowling, some smoke-free, six sand volleyball courts, a huge arcade, go-karts and 18 holes of miniature golf. It's a great place for birthday parties and family gatherings. **Ages: All. Fee.**

Belton-Grandview and Kansas City Railroad, 502 Walnut, Belton, MO 64012-2516, 816-331-0630, www.orgsites.com/mo/beltonrailroad. This train was used in the movie "Biloxi Blues," so you might want to watch that movie with the kids before or after this ride on the authentic 1920 open-air coach. Trains run every Saturday and Sunday at 2 p.m., rain or shine, except for special excursions on Halloween, Memorial Day, Mother's Day, Father's Day and Grandparents. Day. Kids under three ride free. **Ages: All. Fee.**

Belton City Hall Museum, 512 Main St., Belton, MO 64012, 816-322-3977. Housed in the original Belton City Hall, this museum features Native American artifacts and arrows from pioneer days. Kids can see exhibits about famous personalities like Harry Truman. **Ages: All. Free.**

The Berry Patch, 22509 State Line Rd., Cleveland, MO 64734, 816-618-3771. More than two acres of strawberries and miles and miles of blueberry bushes can keep you and your kids busy from mid-May to late August. Read aloud the book *"Blueberries for Sal"* by Robert McCloskey before or after visiting. **Ages: All. Fee.**

Dunn's Cider Mill, 17003 Holmes, Belton, MO 64012, 816-331-7214, www.dunnscidermill.com. Enjoy free samples of delicious natural cider and watch apples being pressed at the mill during apple season. Other treats include cider donuts made fresh daily. Lunch is available Tuesday through Saturday. Ask about the Scarecrow Contest for kids around Halloween and the Johnny Appleseed show. **Ages: All. Fee.**

Landmark 2 Skate Center, U.S. 291 and Hwy. 50, Lee's Summit, MO 64063, 816-524-2000, www.landmark2skate.com. This rink offers a Wednesday night family discount skate night, as well as beginner's skate classes, birthday parties and private parties. **Ages: toddlers and up. Fee**.

Lee's Summit Railroad Station, 220 S. Main St., Lee's Summit, MO 64063. Amtrak provides service from Lee's Summit to Union Station and Science City. You and your child could hop aboard just for fun and have someone pick you up on the other end or take the return train back after exploring Union Station and Crown Center for a few hours. **Ages: All. Fee.**

Gymboree Play and Music of Kansas City, 1587 N.E. Rice Rd., Lee's Summit, MO 64086, 913-469-1118. A full line-up of classes that include music, art and playtime are designed to meet the growing skills and interests of kids. New challenges and experiences take place each week. Baby-sign language is a new addition to the curriculum. **Ages: Birth to 6. Fee.**

Laser Mania, 1051 S.E. Century Dr., Lee's Summit, MO 64081, 816-554-6264, www.lasermania.com/kc**.** For the ultimate laser tag experience, check out the game options in this arena setting open seven days a week. **Ages: 5 and up. Fee.**

Paradise Park Family Entertainment Center, 1021 N.E. Colbern Rd., Lee's Summit, MO 64086, 816-246-5224, www.paradise-park.com**.** This family entertainment center has undergone major renovations in recent years to include an "edutainment" center for children ages 1-9. This includes an art studio, pretend village, water play, children's cooking and block play. Outdoors, the younger kids have a dinosaur dig, pretend fishing and pedal go-karts. For older kids, there's a rock wall, bumper cars and go-karts, mini golf, and batting cages. **Ages: All. Fee.**

Potter's Haven, 224 S.W. Main St., Lee's Summit, MO 64063, 816-525-9323. Located in the former Bank of Lee's Summit building, across the street from the Amtrak station, this family-owned business is a center of creativity for all ages. Grandpa Calvin Bennett teaches lessons on the potter's wheel and encourages any variety of color combinations for children to work with. A monthly Kid's Night is a great opportunity for parents to spend a little time with the kids, then sneak out for some quality time of their own. Birthday parties include karaoke and stuffed animal creations. **Ages: 5 and up. Fee.**

Premiere Bowling and Recreation Center, 11400 E. 350 Hwy., Raytown, MO, 64138, 816-356-5955. Dozens of kids participate in the youth bowling leagues here, and then afterwards enjoy the huge video arcade and the prizes offered. Rock 'n Bowl is a part of the Friday night fun. **Ages: 1st grade and up. Fee.**

Raytown Museum, 9705 E. 63rd St., Raytown, MO 64133, 816-353-5033. A part of the Raytown Historical Society, this museum is housed in a former fire station where exhibits date to the early 1800s. There's a general store and blacksmith shop as well as displays that include a classroom with old desks, books and lunch boxes. **Ages: Preschool and up. Free.**

Super Splash USA, 53rd Place and Raytown Rd., Raytown, MO 64133, 816-356-5300. Three pools, seven slides, sun decks and a family changing room make this a great place for families in the warm weather months. **Ages: All. Fee.**

Skateland of Grandview, 13613 S. U.S. 71, Grandview, MO 64030, 816-763-3220. Entertaining area families since the 1970s, this skating rink has organized family nights and is a good location for birthday parties. The rink has a concrete floor, video games and a snack bar. **Ages: Preschool and up. Fee.**

Summit Fitness, 178 N. Oldham Pkwy., Lee's Summit, MO 64081, 816-525-5040. After school and weekend fitness programs, summer basketball camps, batting cages, a climbing wall and birthday parties are a part of the programs to keep kids here in shape. **Ages: All. Fee.**

Sylvia Bailey Farm Park, 1800 S.E. Ranson Rd., Lee's Summit, MO, 816-969-7756. A historic farm home is the location for agri-educational programming for kids. In the fall, a 12-acre corn maze and hayrides are among the activities for children, sponsored by Lee's Summit Parks and Recreation. **Ages: All. Fee.**

WHO WAS THE LEE IN LEE'S SUMMIT?

TWO STORIES EXIST REGARDING THE LEE IN LEE'S SUMMIT. ONE IS THAT THE CITY'S FOUNDER, A CONFEDERATE SYMPATHIZER, NAMED IT AFTER GENERAL ROBERT E. LEE. THE OTHER IS THAT THE RAILROAD WORKERS WHO WERE SURVEYING IN THE AREA WORKED FROM THE PROPERTY OF DR. PLEASANT LEA AND MISSPELLED HIS NAME WHEN DOCUMENTING THE SITE. EITHER WAY, LEE'S SUMMIT IS THE HIGHEST SUMMIT OVER WHICH THE RAILROADS PASS BETWEEN ST. LOUIS AND LAWRENCE, KS.

Truman Farm Home National Historic Site, 12301 Blue Ridge Blvd., Grandview, MO 64030, 816-254-2720, www.nps.gov/hstr. This was President Harry S Truman's home from 1906 to 1971. Children are usually fascinated by the ceramic chamber pots, since they can't imagine a home without indoor plumbing. Ask about the Junior Ranger Activity Program book for kids 5 to 12. **Ages: All. Fee.**

Tunnel Town, 291 and 50 Hwy., Lee's Summit, MO 64086, 816-524, 2002. When the little ones just need to burn off some energy, this is a creative place filled with tunnels, slides, balls and a climbing wall that appeals to older kids. It's a great place for birthday parties. **Ages: Infant to 12. Fee.**

Unity Village, 350 Hwy. and Colbern Rd., Unity Village, MO 64065, 816-524-3550, www.unityworldhdq.org**.** Unity Village is the headquarters for a non-denominational religious education organization. The village is located in a pleasant park-like setting. There's an activity center, library, rose garden and special programming for children. **Ages: All. Free.**

FUN FOOD AND TREATS

A Sweet Expression, 28 S.E. Third St., Lee's Summit, MO 64063, 816-347-8400, www.asweetexpression.com**.** More than just an ice cream store, you and the kids will drool over the fudge counter, the cookie bouquets and the fun gift items for family and friends.

Fox's Drug Store 10004 E. 63rd St., Raytown, MO 64133, 816-353-1600. This family-owned drugstore still has a delightful soda fountain where you can get great ice cream treats and sandwiches.

Did you know?

Adams Dairy Parkway is named for the dairy operation that was centered at R.D. Mize Road and Adams Dairy Parkway, which was once the largest dairy operating in the state of Missouri. A mini-museum of what the dairy looked like is in the lobby of the office building on the southwest corner of the intersection.

Fun House Pizza and Pub, 9120 E. 350 Hwy., Raytown, MO 64133, 816-356-5141, www.funhousepizza.com. In addition to pizza, this restaurant keeps the kids entertained with a merry-go-round, videos, television and rides. Kids can watch the pizza being made.

Just Desserts, 13 S.W. Third St., Lee's Summit, MO 64063, 816-554-6940. Located in the old Lee's Summit Fire Station, just one block from the Amtrak station, this sweet spot is filled with train and fire memorabilia, as well as a huge collection of cookie jars.

SPECIAL SHOPS

Ingenious Toystore, 218 N. Oldham Pkwy., Lee's Summit, MO 64081, 816-524-3838. One of the larger specialty toy stores in the metropolitan area, here you'll find some of the most educational and creative products on the market to stimulate your child's development.

A LITTLE FARTHER OUT

Lone Jack Civil War Battlefield and Cemetery, 301 S. Bynum Rd., (1 block south of U.S. 50 at Lone Jack exit). 816-697-8833. You can't pass up an opportunity to teach the kids a little Civil War history, particularly when it's in our backyard. This is the site of the August 16, 1862 battle of hand-to-hand fighting between Union and Confederate troops. A commemoration is held the weekend closest to the original battle date. **Ages: 1st grade and up. Fee.**

TRIVIA

JAMES A. REED WAS MAYOR OF KANSAS CITY FROM 1900-1904 AND U.S. SENATOR FROM 1911 TO 1929. HE ALSO SOUGHT THE DEMOCRATIC NOMINATION FOR PRESIDENT IN 1928 AND 1932. A ROADWAY THROUGH LEE'S SUMMIT IS NAMED IN HIS HONOR AS WELL AS A WILDLIFE AREA.

Clay County, MO

Includes Kansas City, North Kansas City, Gladstone, Kearney, Excelsior Springs, Smithville and Liberty.

Welcome

Kansas City, North Kansas City, and Gladstone

Northland Regional Chamber of Commerce, 634 N.W. Englewood Rd., Kansas City, MO 64118, 816-455-9911, www.northlandchamber.com. This organization offers a number of college scholarships to Clay and Platte County residents.

Gladstone Chamber of Commerce, 6504 N. Oak, Gladstone, MO 64118, 816-436-4523, www.gladstonechamber.com.

Assistance

Children's Mercy North Community Education, 816-413-2500. Programs are offered at your request and designed to meet the needs and age of your group on any health or safety topic, from washing hands to burn issues to water safety.

Teen Yellow Pages/Parent Yellow Pages, 816-468-7088, ext. 308, www.tri-countrymhs.org. This pocket-sized directory, distributed at no charge by the Clay, Platte and Ray Mental Health Board of Trustees, provides information about area non-profit organizations that can help teens or their parents with issues such as eating disorders, substance abuse, domestic violence and pregnancy.

Mothers and More, Northland, www.kcnorthmothersandmore.homestead. com. This group of women who altered career paths for their children meet at the Barry Christian Church, 1500 N.W. Barry Rd., on the second and fourth Tuesdays of the month.

Northland Therapeutic Riding Center, Kearney, MO 816-472-1855, www.northlandtrc.org. This non-profit center helps children with a number of physical, mental and emotional challenges by introducing them to the companionship of horses.

Community Centers

Gladstone Community Center, 800 N.E. 69th St., Gladstone, MO 64118, 816-436-2200. Located in Central Park, this center has a large community kitchen and restroom facilities for the park.

Kansas City North Community Center, 3930 N.E. Antioch Rd., Kansas City, MO 64117, 816-784-6100. The center holds year-round children's classes offering arts and crafts, and martial arts as well as girls volleyball leagues.

North Kansas City Community Center, 1999 Iron St., North Kansas City, MO 64116, 816-300-0531, www.nkccc.org. This great facility has a little bit of everything – a rock climbing wall, an indoor lap-swim pool and river walk, an indoor kids water park with slides and fountains, a large gym and fun activities through the year.

Sherwood Family Recreation Center, 4900 N. Norton, Kansas City, MO 64119, 816-452-4457. Owned by the Sherwood Bible Church, this family-oriented facility welcomes all members of the community. The center offers lighted tennis courts, volleyball and basketball courts, and an Olympic-size pool. There's a swim team and tennis lessons for people of all ages. No smoking is allowed on the premises and some dress codes apply.

THE GREAT OUTDOORS

Gladstone Parks and Recreation, 7010 N. Holmes, Gladstone, MO 64118, 816-436-2200, www.gladstone.mo.us**.** Of the city's many youth programs, basketball is the most popular with more than 1,000 children participating on organized teams.

Kansas City, Missouri Parks and Recreation, 4600 E. 63rd St., Kansas City, MO 64130, 816-513-7500, www.kcmo.org**.**

North Kansas City Parks and Recreation, 1999 Iron St., North Kansas City, MO 64116, 816-300-0545, www.nkc.org**.** In addition to extremely popular soccer, baseball, and t-ball leagues, this city department invites children from around the metro to its Summer Jamboree in Macken Park in August and its Halloween Party in October. Both events are FREE!

SPECIAL AREA PARKS AND PLAYGROUNDS

Anita Gorman Park, Davidson Rd. and N.E. 46th Terr., Kansas City, MO. Named after a Northland resident who has championed the cause of public parks, this 45-acre triangular park contains a massive public fountain that freezes over in the winter, creating a fascinating ice sculpture that changes with the weather. It's particularly beautiful at night when colored lights show through the water and ice.

Central Park, 69th and N. Holmes, Gladstone, MO 816-436-2200 (pool only). This 14-acre park is home to three public swimming pools that include a baby pool, an intermediate pool and a T-shaped adult pool. The park also has tennis courts, modern restrooms and a playground. Central Park is also home to the Gladstone Teacher Memorial and a special memorial to the Space Shuttle Challenger's teacher Christa McAuliffe.

Children's Fountain, 9 Hwy. and N. Oak Trafficway, North Kansas City. The image that graces the cover of this edition of *A Kid's Guide to Kansas City* was added to the Kansas City fountain assembly in 1995. It celebrates the spirit of children in six dancing figures in a pool of water. Honor your child by purchasing a brick on the walkway by calling 816-842-2299.

Dagg Park, 21st and Howell St., North Kansas City, MO. This small park has a free wading pool with sprayer jets and another fountain open for kids to run through on hot summer days.

Hodge Park, 7000 N.E. Barry Rd., Kansas City, MO. This 1,029-acre park includes a golf course, picnic sites, ballfields, and remote controlled airplane field, but is most known for Shoal Creek Living History Museum, a reconstructed town that features authentic pioneer log cabin homes, a grist mill, plantation estate, school house, church, jail and general store. Nearby is a fenced area where buffalo and elk roam. Each November, the park is the site of the Wilderness Run that allows families to jog through the woodlands and end up in the Living History village.

Macken Park, Howell & Clark Fergusson Dr., North Kansas City, MO. This 60-acre park is the site of many of the city's largest gatherings and sporting events. In addition to a paved walking trail, Macken Park has a paved roller-blading trail, a totlap playground and a wheelchair swing.

Maple Woods Nature Preserve, N. Prospect and 76th St., Gladstone, MO 64118, 816-436-2200. This state-owned area, operated by the city of Gladstone, is a mystery. The pristine forest is the largest stand of sugar maples west of the Mississippi River, far from the northern climates where these trees are found. About 45 acres are home to deer, raccoons, skunks, possums, birds and bugs. There are picnic tables in the parking lot and six miles of nature trails to roam.

Oak Grove Park, 76th and N. Troost, Gladstone, MO. Oak trees fill this 17-acre park that is home to the city's summer theatre program. The park also has a modern playground, sand volleyball courts and a half-mile paved walking trail.

Penguin Park, N. Vivion Rd. and N. Norton, Kansas City, MO, 816-513-7500. Huge fiberglass animals dot the playground here, including a super-sized kangaroo, elephant and penguin. In the winter, the park is converted to a Santa's Wonderland. The enclosed shelter may be reserved for birthday parties year round.

Pleasant Valley Park & Athletic Complex, 6401 N.E. Pleasant Valley Dr., Kansas City, MO. The skateboard park located here is often host to free lessons and demonstrations from leaders in the sport.

THINGS TO DO

AMF Pro-Bowl, 505 E. 18th Ave., North Kansas City, MO 64116, 816-221-8844, www.probowllanes.amfcenters.com**.** Bowling is just a part of the fun here that includes go-karts, batting cages, mini-golf and video games. **Ages: All. Fee.**

Athletic and Golf Club at Maple Creek, 5330 N.E. Oak Ridge Rd., Kansas City, MO 64119, 816-459-8400. Tucked away on a tree-covered hillside, this facility has 36 holes of miniature golf, as well as a nine-hole executive golf course along with a 6,000 square foot family fitness center. **Ages: 2 and up. Fee**.

Cornfield Maze, North Oak Trafficway and 102nd Terr., Kansas City, MO, 816-734-4183. This acre of geometric fun is best for smaller kids. Open seasonally from about mid-July when the corn gets tall enough until a late harvest in November, this maze has 20 dead-ends and lots of fun features. **Ages: All. Fee.**

Once there was Winnwood Beach

Long before the days of Worlds of Fun, the Northland boasted Winnwood Beach, a huge amusement park/water playground located where the Chouteau Crossing Shopping Center now stands at I-35 and Northeast Choteau Trafficway. Often called "The Atlantic City of the West," the park operated from 1913 to 1940 entertaining up to 5,000 visitors a day. Winnwood Beach, named for owners Frank and Janet Winn, included three lakes, two roller coasters, a huge bathhouse, a boardwalk and a sand beach, a zoo and funhouse. A historic marker in the shopping center today tells the story of fun times long ago.

Laser Storm Family Adventure, Antioch and Vivion Rd., Gladstone, MO 64119, 816-452-8081, www.laserstormkc.net. Located in the lower level of Antioch Mall, this is an indoor laser tag arena with barriers and objects for players to hide behind. It's black-lit to add to the challenge of hitting your opponent with laser lights. There's also an arcade and private birthday party room. **Ages: 5 and up. Fee.**

Fins and Foliage Pet Store, 7022 N. Locust, Gladstone, MO 64118, 816-436-6062, www.finsandfoliage.com. Kids can play with a puppy, pet a guinea pig, tour a fish room and talk to birds on the educational tour of this large pet store. **Ages: Preschool and up. Free.**

Gladstone Bowl, 300 N.W. 72nd St., Gladstone, MO 64118, 816-436-2695, www.gladstonebowl.com. Galactic bowling on Saturday afternoons and evenings, in a smoke-free environment, is a great family activity here and a popular birthday party outing. League bowling is available for those three and up. **Ages: 3 and up. Fee.**

Gladstone Theatre in the Park, 816-436-2200, www.gladstone.mo.us. This Northland institution provides a family-type stage production in July and August in Oak Grove Park at 76th and N. Troost. Most productions have children in the cast. Check the city website for scheduled performances. **Ages: All. Fee.**

Holiday Mini-Golf, 5006 N.E. Parvin Rd., Kansas City, MO 64117, 816-452-2408. An indoor 12-hole mini-golf course, along with a video and billiards room, make this a great hang-out and birthday party site throughout the year. **Ages: All. Fee.**

Jaegers Subsurface Paintball, 9300 N.E. Underground, Kansas City, MO 64161, 816-452-6600, www.jaegers.com. The area's only underground paintball field, Jaeger's is located in the limestone caves where temperatures are a constant 56 degrees, so dress warmly. There's also an above ground field. **Ages: 10 and up. Fee.**

Scuba Adventures, 5100 N.E. Chouteau Trafficway, Kansas City, MO 64119, 816-455-1492, www.scubad.com**.** "Discover Scuba" is a program that allows kids to experience a one-time dive in a local pool. An Adventuring Crew club, for kids 14 and up, is a club for all water sports. Family rates and lessons are available. **Ages: 10 and up. Fee.**

The Q, 6829 N. Oak Trafficway, Gladstone, MO 64118, 816-468-0100. This family-friendly, smoke-free environment is open to all ages through out the week, but is reserved for middle schoolers on Friday night and teenagers on Saturday night. The Q offers billiards, food, and music with a DJ. There is a dress code and security on the premises. **Ages: All, Friday night, 13-15, Saturday night, 15-20 only. Fee.**

Worlds of Fun/Oceans of Fun 4545 Worlds of Fun Dr., Kansas City, MO 64161, 816-454-4545, www.worldsoffun.com**.** This 235-acre park is a family vacation unto itself. In fact, many families travel to Kansas City specifically to visit these two properties, where camping was added in 2005. Worlds of Fun has more than 50 rides and attractions, but is best known for the 12-story tall roller coaster called the Boomerang and one of the world's top-rated wooden roller coasters called the Timberwolf. Less adventurous rides are available through Camp Snoopy, a one-acre mini-park with rides and attractions designed especially for families with small children. Food is available inside the park but a shaded picnic area outside the park is a popular and less expensive alternative.

Oceans of Fun is the largest water park in the Midwest that includes everything from slides and wave pools to kayaking and sunning. The whole family enjoys the Hurricane Falls raft ride and the Surf City wave pool when "Wipe-Out" signals the heightened surf waves. Smaller children enjoy the Captain Kidd's pirate ship and sprayers, while the bigger kids can burn off hours of energy attempting to cross Crocodile Isle. Inner tubes are available for daily rental. **Ages: There is no age limit for either park, but height restrictions apply. A discounted one-day admission to both parks is available.**

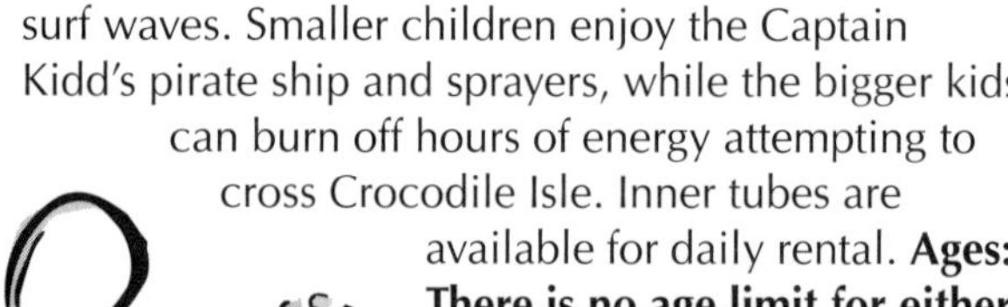

FUN FOOD AND TREATS

Chappell's Restaurant and Sports Museum, 323 Armour Rd., North Kansas City, MO 64116, 816-421-0002. Better than any sports Hall of Fame, Chappell's is filled with every imaginable sport item once owned by some of the most prestigious athletes. While ogling the ceiling exhibits, remember to keep a heads up for some of Kansas City's sports celebrities who often eat here. By the way, the food's pretty good and they have a kids' menu. Kids are also given a great souvenir.

Stroud's Oak Ridge Manor, 5410 N.E. Oak Ridge Dr., Kansas City, MO 64119, 816-454-9600, www.stroudsrestaurant.com**.** This historic home dates to1829 and is now a popular restaurant famous for its fried chicken, mashed potatoes and cinnamon rolls served family-style. Before or after you eat, stroll the grounds, feeding the ducks and fish in the pond.

The Sweet Tooth, 1909 Swift, North Kansas City, MO 64116, 816-221-2428. You have trouble getting the kids to brush their teeth? Try a chocolate toothbrush. That's one of the many fun items available in this independent little shop that carries such old-fashioned favorites as waxed lips and all 21 colors of M&Ms.

KEARNEY, EXCELSIOR SPRINGS, SMITHVILLE

WELCOME

Excelsior Springs Chamber of Commerce, 101 E. Broadway, Excelsior Springs, MO 64204, 816-630-6161,
www.exspgschamber.com *Look at the tourism section of the website.*

> ENJOY DINNER TOGETHER
>
> CHILDREN WHO SIT DOWN FOR DINNER WITH THE FAMILY A COUPLE OF TIMES A WEEK DO BETTER IN SCHOOL, ARE HEALTHIER PEOPLE AND ARE LESS LIKELY TO DRINK, SMOKE OR USE DRUGS, ACCORDING TO A UNIVERSITY OF MICHIGAN STUDY.

Kearney Chamber of Commerce, 100 E. Washington St., Kearney, MO 64060, 816-628-4229, www.kearneymo.com.

Smithville Chamber of Commerce, P.O. Box 61, Smithville, MO 64089, 816-532-0946.

SPECIAL AREA PARKS AND PLAYGROUNDS

Little Platte Park, Smithville, 816-532-0803. Located on the west side of the lake, this small park includes a working replica of the only known prehistoric Native American solar calendar. The original site was flooded when Smithville Lake was created in the 1970s. One of the lake's marinas and swim beaches is located here.

Smithville Lake, Two miles east of U.S. 169, Smithville, MO 64089, 816-532-0803. Located amid rolling hills and grassland, the 7,200-acre lake is surrounded by 27 miles of partially-paved walking and biking trails, along with another 10 miles of horseback riding trails. The recreation areas include more than 777 campsites for tents and RVs, two swimming beaches, 200 picnic sites, 11 shelter houses and two full-service marinas. There are also two golf courses (816-532-4100) and a trap and skeet-shooting field. A handicapped accessible fishing dock is also a part of the facility.

Tryst Falls Park, five miles east of Kearny on Hwy. 92, 816-532-0803. This 40-acre park includes the area's only waterfall open to the public. It's a great place to picnic, but fishing and swimming are not allowed.

Watkins Woolen Mill State Park, 816-580-3387, www.mostateparks.com/wwmill **or** www.watkinsmill.org**.** Located 6.5 miles north of Excelsior Springs and 7 miles east of Kearney on Hwy. 92, this is the last 19th century woolen mill in the United States with original equipment. The mill contains 60 of the original machines and a steam engine. The Watkins home, smokehouse, summer kitchen and fruit drying house, along with an octagonal school and church, remain. Tours are available. Native livestock, including sheep, chickens and turkeys, live at the farm. The park is a great place to picnic, camp, ride bikes, fish and swim.

THINGS TO DO

American Italian Pasta Co., 1000 Italian Way, Excelsior Springs, MO 64024, 816-502-6219 or 816-584-5000, www.pastalabella.com. You'll find Pasta LaBella on the shelves of most area grocery stores, but you'll see it made during a 40-minute tour that includes the big presses that shape the pasta and the dryers that get it ready for packaging. It's hot in here and in the summer, you can't wear shorts or sandals, because it is a food production facility. **Ages: 13 and up. Free.**

The Elms Resort, 401 Regent St., Excelsior Springs, MO 64024, 816-630-5500, www.elmsresort.com. One of the most historic sites in metropolitan Kansas City, this is where Harry Truman was the night he found out he had been elected president. Today, the Elms is often considered a romantic escape for couples, which is true, but there are also family packages to enjoy the indoor and outdoor pools, the 16 miles of biking trails, volleyball courts and open gym. **Ages: All. Fee.**

Excelsior Springs Historical Museum, 101 E. Broadway, Excelsior Springs, MO 64024, 816-630-6161. Located in the former Clay County Bank building, this is a place where you can learn about "The Valley of Vitality," what the Native Americans once called the spring waters of Excelsior Springs. In addition to historic records and videos, there are many displays of the unusual water bottling processes used over the years. **Ages: All. Free.**

Hall of Waters, 201 E. Broadway, Excelsior Springs, MO 64204, 816-630-0753, www.hallofwaters.com. The central point of the city revered for the healing powers of its water is the Hall of Waters and the world's longest water bar. The kids can have a soft drink, but everyone should appreciate the fresco art on the ceilings. **Ages: All. Fee for purchases.**

Jerry Litton Visitor Center, south end of Smithville Lake, 816-532-0174. Named for a former sixth district congressman, this Army Corps of Engineers center has exhibits and artifacts on the Missouri Valley and the Native Americans who inhabited it. The center includes nature films and schedules tours of the dam. **Ages: All. Free.**

Jesse James Farm and Museum, 21216 James Farm Rd., two miles east of Kearney on Hwy. 92, Kearney, MO 64060, 816-628-6065, www.jessejames.org**.** This is the birthplace of legendary train/bank robber Jesse James, where he and his brother Frank grew up during the mid-1800s. The house has been authentically restored and the museum includes the world's largest collection of James family artifacts. It is open year-round. **Ages: All. Fee.**

Jesse James Grave, Mount Olivet Cemetery, west of Kearney on Hwy. 92. Jesse's grave is located near two small evergreen trees on the cemetery's west side. Originally, he was buried on the front lawn of the farm so that his family could protect his remains, but the grave was later moved to the public cemetery. His remains have been exhumed for DNA and other testing to prove their authenticity.
(Note: Fans of Jesse James history may wish to visit St. Joseph, Missouri and the Jesse James Home Museum at 12th & Penn Street. This is where James was living at the time he was killed by a former member of his own gang. Suggested reading: Shifra Stein's Day Trips® from Kansas City)

Mount Gilead Church and School, 15918 Plattsburg Rd., Kearney, MO 64060, 816-628-6065. This is the only one-room schoolhouse west of the Mississippi River to have remained open during the Civil War. Clay County schedules half-day-long classes for children to participate in, complete with a school marm and McGuffey's Readers. A 38-star American flag flies in front. Reservations required. **Ages: 3rd grade and 4th grade only. Fee.**

FUN FOOD AND TREATS

Kookies, 601 S. Jefferson St., Kearney, MO 64060, 816-628-5720. In addition to great pizza, this small-town restaurant has a video game room and ball play area for the kids.

Wabash BBQ, 646 S. Kansas City Ave., Excelsior Springs, MO 64024, 816-630-7700, www.wabashbbq.com**.** Located in a historic train depot across from the Elms, the eatery has a fun décor and great food.

Special Shops

All About Books, 14461 N. 169 Highway, Smithville, MO 64089, 816-532-9959. This full-service, independent bookstore offers monthly story times for kids and fun holiday and themed events for the kids. Ask about teacher discounts and fundraising opportunities.

Liberty

Welcome

Liberty Area Chamber of Commerce, 9 S. Leonard St., Liberty, MO 64068, 816-781-5200, www.libertychamber.com.

Community Centers

Liberty Community Center, 1600 S. Withers Rd., Liberty, MO 64068, 816-792-6009, www.ci.liberty.mo.us. This impressive center has four swimming pools, two in and two out, one of which is a therapy pool with handicap access. There's also a billiards room, work-out area, sauna and whirlpool. This is also the home of the Liberty Performing Arts Theatre.

The Great Outdoors

Liberty Parks and Recreation Department, 1600 S. Withers Rd., Liberty, MO 64068, 816-792-6081. In addition to many traditional sports offerings for kids, this city department offers karate, judo, tap and ballet for youth.

Special Area Parks and Playgrounds

Bennett Park, 1100 Clayview St., (north of Hwy. 152), Liberty. This 45-acre park features a skateboard park, an amphitheatre, tennis and volleyball courts, a concession stand and fitness trail.

City Park, 970 S. Hwy. 291, Liberty. A sprayground keeps kids cool in the summer and a great playground and ballfields keep them active the rest of the year.

Martha Lafite Thompson Nature Sanctuary, 407 N. LaFrenz Rd., Liberty, MO 64068, 816-781-8598, www.naturesanctuary.com**.** This 100-acre sanctuary is filled with wildlife that inhabits prairies, woodlands, meadows and marshes. White-tailed deer, raccoons, foxes, squirrels, birds and butterflies delight kids of all ages during outings on the many walking trails. The visitor center features educational exhibits and hosts organized activities such as wildflower and full-moon hikes.

THINGS TO DO

Clay County Museum, 14 N. Main St., Liberty, MO 64068, 816-792-1849. Housed in an 1877 drug store, the museum collection features a restored doctor's office, prehistoric Native American relics, toys, tools, arrowheads and other artifacts. **Ages: All. Fee.**

James A. Rooney Justice Center, 11 S. Water St., Liberty, MO 64068, 816-792-7612. The north side of the courthouse features ceramic murals that tell the county's history. Ask for brochures that interpret the murals inside the courthouse. Tours are available inside and may include a visit with a judge, if scheduling permits. If court is in session, children may sit in, but they must be quiet. **Ages: 1st grade and up. Free.**

TRIVIA

ALEXANDER DONIPHAN IS A NAME THAT APPEARS ON SCHOOLS, HIGHWAYS AND OTHER SITES AROUND CLAY COUNTY. HE WAS A MEMBER OF THE STATE LEGISLATURE AND MILITIA IN THE EARLY DAYS OF MISSOURI STATEHOOD. DONIPHAN WAS ORDERED BY THE GOVERNOR TO ARREST MORMON LEADER JOSEPH SMITH, IMPRISON HIM IN LIBERTY AND EXECUTE HIM. DONIPHAN REFUSED TO CARRY OUT THE EXECUTION.

Jesse James Bank Museum, 103 N. Water St., Liberty, MO 64068, 816-781-4458. Frank and Jesse James were responsible for the first successful daylight bank robbery during peace time and this is where they did it, "withdrawing" $60,000 on February 13, 1866. The building is on the National Register of Historic Places. The bank also tells the story of the history and process of banking. **Ages: All. Fee for those over 8 years old.**

Go-Kart Track, on H Hwy., one mile east of Liberty, 816-737-5647, www.kcka.com. Since the 1960s, children and adults have been racing homemade and commercial go-carts on this asphalt track. Competitive races are held every other Sunday during warm weather, but you can ride for fun the rest of the time. **Ages: 5 and up. Fee.**

Historic Liberty Jail, 216 N. Main St., Liberty, MO 64068, 816-781-3188. Otherwise known as the Mormon Jail, this is where Mormon leader Joseph Smith was imprisoned for his religious beliefs in 1838. The jail has cutaway walls so kids can see what conditions were like more than 175 years ago. The visitors' center teaches about the unfairness of persecuting those of different faiths and beliefs. **Ages: Preschool and up. Free.**

Liberty Farmers' Market, west side of Liberty Square, Liberty, MO, 816-781-2649. The Saturday market is open from early mornings May through October and you can find a variety of produce grown by local farmers. **Ages: All. Fee for purchases.**

Liberty Hospital Teddy Bear Tour, 2525 Glenn Hendren Dr., Liberty, MO 64068, 816-781-7200, www.libertyhospital.org. Children on this tour begin by receiving a doctor or nurse's hat, then tour the hospital where they can work the controls on a hospital bed, see broken bones in radiology and ooh and aah over the babies in the nursery. In the end, their favorite stuffed animal receives a shot, and the kids get a goodie bag to take home. **Ages: 4 to 6. Free.**

Liberty Performing Arts Theatre, 1600 Withers Rd., Liberty, MO 64068, 816-792-6130, www.lpat.org. This professional theatre group produces as many as eight children's events throughout the year. Check the website for shows, times and age appropriateness. **Ages: Preschool and up. Fee.**

Mabee Center, William Jewell College, Liberty, MO 64068, 816-781-7700, ext. 5294, www.william.jewell.edu. The Mabee Center has an Olympic-size indoor pool, as well as racquetball and basketball courts for rent. Family swims are available at the pool. In summer, the center hosts volleyball, basketball and football camps for the kids. **Ages: All. Fee.**

Northland Rolladium, 1020 Kent St., Liberty, MO 64068, 816-792-0590. This roller skating rink features family skate night on Saturday night and is also available for private parties. Special sessions and lessons are available for young skaters. **Ages: All. Fee.**

FUN FOOD AND TREATS

Hardware Café, 5 E. Kansas St., Liberty, MO 64068, 816-792-3500, www.thehardwarecafe.com. Once the home of an old-time hardware store, the café is now a wonderful ice cream shop and a great place for fun lunches and desserts.

Scoops Frozen Custard and Ice Cream, 18 N. Main St., Liberty, MO 64068, 816-415-8557. Have a birthday party here or just drop in for popcorn, a hot dog or one of more than a dozen flavors of frozen custard and hard ice cream.

SPECIAL SHOPS

By the Book, 4 N. Main St., Liberty, MO 64068, 816-792-3200. This locally-owned bookstore is a great place to find new and used children's books, as well as kids games and plush toys. They also have a coffee bar with fun milk shakes and frozen drinks for kids.

Cradle to Crayons, 129 S. Stewart, Liberty, MO 64068, 816-792-2712, www.cradletocrayons.com. In addition to some really fun children's clothes for sale, this imaginative store also has a party room that is appropriate for children's teas, birthdays or even a baby shower.

A LITTLE FARTHER NORTH

Shatto Milk Company, 9406 N. Hwy. 33, Osborn, MO 64474, 816-930-3862, www.shattomilkcompany.com. Head north out of Smithville on Hwy. 169 or keep going on I-35 past Liberty. Either way, you are looking for Highway 116, which intersects with Hwy. 33, where you'll find signs for Shatto Milk, a family-owned dairy that still bottles in glass bottles and produces hormone free milk. A tour of the family farm is a treat for those of all ages. Kids may get to bottle feed the newborn calves, but everyone will see how the cows live, eat and play. Enjoy a fresh-baked chocolate chip cookie and a glass of cold milk at the end of the tour. Check the website for special events. **Ages: All. Fee.**

WHO WAS THE SMITH OF SMITHVILLE?

HUMPHREY SMITH CAME TO CLAY COUNTY IN 1822 AND BUILT THE FIRST GRAIN MILL NORTH OF THE MISSOURI RIVER ON THE LITTLE PLATTE. THE TOWN THAT DEVELOPED WAS KNOWN AS SMITH'S FORK, BUT SOMETIME LATER WAS INCORPORATED AS SMITH'S MILL AND THEN LATER SMITHVILLE.

Platte County, MO

Includes Kansas City, Parkville, Platte City, Riverside and Weston

Welcome

Platte County-KCI Area Convention and Visitors Bureau, 11724 N.W. Plaza Circle, # 200, Kansas City, MO 64153, 816-270-3979 or 888-875-2883, www.co.platte.mo.us**.**

Kansas City, Riverside, Parkville

Welcome

Main Street Parkville Association, 8701 N.W. Riverpark Dr., Parkville, MO 64152, 816-505-2227, www.parkvillemo.com**.**

Riverside Area Chamber of Commerce, 4617 N.W. Gateway, Riverside, MO 64150, 816-746-1577, www.riversidekc.com**.**

Assistance

Park Hill Community Drug Task Force, 7301 N.W. Barry Rd., Kansas City, MO 64152, 816-741-1521. This organization hosts a number of family and teen events throughout the year to provide alternatives for drug and alcohol use among young people.

Parents as Teachers, 7301 N.W. Barry Rd., Kansas City, MO 64152, 816-741-3884. Vision, hearing and physical development evaluation screenings are an important and free part of this program. Parents can learn to teach their kids through activities at home. Prenatal brain development strategies are available as well. **Ages: Prenatal to 5.**

COMMUNITY CENTERS

Heartland Presbyterian Center, 16965 N.W. Hwy. 45, Parkville, MO 64152, 816-891-1078. A popular retreat for scout and church camps, this center is also available for family sleep-overs. There are horseback riding and hiking trails.

Line Creek Community Center, Ice Arena and Park, 5940 N.W. Waukomis Dr., Kansas City, MO 64151, 816-505-2244. This full-sized indoor ice arena is open year-round and offers figure skating lessons and hockey teams. In the warm months, kids fill the zero depth entry pool. There are also craft and meeting rooms, and a weight room and snack bar.

Parkville Athletic Complex, 6014 N.W. 9 Hwy., Parkville, MO 64152, 816-741-4424. Adjacent to the Platte County South Community Center, this privately-owned center offers indoor practice facilities for soccer, futsal and basketball. There are also batting cages, meeting rooms, video games, locker rooms, and a snack bar.

Platte County South Community Center, 8875 Clark Ave., Parkville, MO 64152, 816-561-9622. New to the community in the spring of 2005, this center includes a zero-entry swimming pool, water slide and outdoor sprayground, as well as indoor and outdoor play adventure centers for kids. The kitchen is designed as a teaching center as well.

THE GREAT OUTDOORS

Kansas City, Missouri Parks and Recreations, 4600 E. 63rd St., Kansas City, MO 64130, 816-513-7500, www.kcmo.org.

SPECIAL AREA PARKS AND PLAYGROUNDS

E. H. Young Riverfront Park, near the Argosy Casino on Tullison Rd., Riverside, 816-741-3993. The beautiful mile-long riverfront walkway and stone amphitheatre are the focal points of this park, named for a long time civic leader who donated the 25 acres. A playground and ball diamond are among the amenities.

English Landing Park, Parkville, 816-741-7676. The center of many activities for the residents of Parkville and those who drive from surrounding communities, English Landing Park boasts a fabulous 3.5-mile gravel path along the Missouri River that is perfect for walking or biking. Two interesting bridges make their home in the park, as well as a modern, shaded playground, batting cages and ball diamond. Kids love to watch the trains go by on the adjacent Burlington-Northern-Santa Fe track.

Parkville Nature Sanctuary, 12th & East St., (behind the city hall) Parkville, 816-741-7676. Waterfalls, wetlands and a scenic overlook are included in the 115-acres filled with walking trails and an old Girl Scout cabin. Special activities throughout the year, such as ghost stories at Halloween and bird watching in the winter, are all great activities for the kids.

Southern Platte Pass. This two-mile asphalt paved walking trail along Highway 45 provides a safe place for riding bikes or walking and will eventually connect to English Landing Park in Parkville and Line Creek Park in Kansas City.

Tiffany Springs Park, N.W. 88th & Hampton Rd., Kansas City, MO. This 66-acre athletic complex is a joint operation between Kansas City Missouri Parks and Recreation and the Southern Platte County Athletic Association. In addition to numerous soccer and baseball fields, the aquatic center has a 50-meter pool, a leisure pool and spraygrounds for the kids.

THINGS TO DO

All Fired Up, 7659 N.W. Prairie View Rd., Kansas City, MO 64151, 816-584-0060, www.justglazeit.com. This paint-your-own pottery store is a great place to stir a child's creativity. Scouts can earn a pottery badge with a tour of the studio. **Ages: 5-12. Fee.**

American Truck Historical Society, 10380 N. Ambassador Dr., # 101, Kansas City, MO 64153, 816-891-9900, www.aths.org. More than 1700 dye-cast antique toy trucks are on display at this center, which includes a library with histories and memorabilia from truck builders and truck lines. **Ages: All. Free.**

Back Yard Bird Center, 6212 NW Barry Rd., Kansas City, MO 64154, 816-746-1113. Located in the Boardwalk Square shops, the store is as much a teaching center about birds and their habitat as it is a supply center for bird seed, feeders and houses. Owner Mark McKellar is a wildlife biologist who is available for programs and other educational outings with children interested in birds.

Chess Club, 2314 N.W. Vivion Rd., Riverside MO 64150, 816-407-7017. The only center like it in Kansas City, the Chess Club is where people of all ages, but especially children come to learn, watch and play the game of chess. Free instruction each Friday evening is followed by tournaments on Saturday. **Ages: All. Fee to play.**

Gymboree, 180 English Landing Dr., Parkville, MO 64152, 913-469-1118. A full line-up of classes that include music, art and playtime are designed to meet the growing skills and interests of kids. New challenges and experiences take place each week. Baby-sign language is a new addition to the curriculum. **Ages: Birth to 6. Fee.**

Harley-Davidson Assembly Plant and Visitors Center, 11401 N. Congress Dr., Kansas City, MO 64153, 877-883-1450, www.harleydavidson.com**.** This is one of two Harley-Davidson motorcycle final assembly plants in the country. The 90-minute walking tour requires reservations for groups of ten or more. **Ages: 12 and older. Free.**

Kansas City Northern Railroad, 5940 N.W. Waukomis Dr., Kansas City, MO 64151, 816-734-0203. Two 16-inch gauge trains, restored and operated by volunteers, run on a half-mile track through tunnels and around the park. Open weekends only. May through September. **Ages: All. Fee.**

Park Hill Aquatic Center, 8152 N. Congress Dr., Kansas City, MO 64152, 816-741-7963. This Olympic-size pool and dive center offers classes and open swim time for people of all ages. The indoor pool is six-lane, 25-meters and includes an outdoor sundeck. The facility is available for birthday parties and other large events**. Ages: All. Fee.**

Parkville Farmers Market, south of the railroad tracks, Parkville, 816-741-7676. From early May to late October, bring the kids to one of the oldest and most diverse farmers markets in the metro. Activities are Saturday morning and Wednesday afternoons. **Ages: All. Fee for purchases.**

"IT'S A PUZZLEMENT"

THE RIVERSIDE BRANCH OF THE MID-CONTINENT PUBLIC LIBRARY, 2700 N.W. VIVION RD., 816-741-6288, IS THE ONLY ONE IN THE SYSTEM TO OFFER JIGSAW PUZZLES FOR CHECK-OUT. THERE ARE MORE THAN 50 CHILDREN'S PUZZLES AVAILABLE TO CHOOSE FROM. CONSIDER MAKING A DONATION OF OLD PUZZLES.

Parkville Mini-Golf, 7 Mill St., Parkville, MO 64152, 816-505-9555, www.parkvilleminigolf.com**.** The view of the Missouri River is fantastic, but kids are probably more focused on this unique 18-hole course that includes uphill holes and lots of humps in the course. The air-conditioned clubhouse serves Blue Bell Ice Cream! **Ages: All. Fee.**

Park University, 8701 N.W. Riverpark Dr., Parkville, MO 64152, 816-741-2000, www.park.edu**.** This beautiful campus was built in the late 1800s by students who hand-hewed the limestone found in many of the buildings. The library is underground and provides an interesting glimpse into the uses of the limestone caverns that are common in the Kansas City area. The view of the Missouri River from Mackay Hall is worth the climb. **Ages: All. Free.**

River Roll Skate Center, 4720 Gateway Dr., Riverside, MO 64150, 816-587-0131, www.riveroll.com**.** This skate center has one of the few wooden floors remaining in metropolitan Kansas City. In-line hockey and speed skating are among the activities available here, but River Roll is also a popular place for birthday parties and school events. It's a non-smoking facility. **Ages: All. Fee.**

In conjunction with River Roll is **Club Mixer**, a dance club for high school students only. On Saturday evening, Mix 93 Radio DJs provide the music and Club Mixer provides a safe environment for teenagers. **Fee. Ages: High School only.**

Riverside Public Pool, 4498 N.W. High Dr., Riverside, MO 64150, 816-587-07801. This small zero-depth entry pool is in a C-shape and is good for smaller children who may be intimidated by the heavy splashing and noise in larger pools. **Ages: All. Fee.**

Summit Athletic Club, 6501 N. Cosby Ave., Kansas City, MO 64151, 816-505-1200. After-school and weekend fitness programs, summer basketball camps, batting cages, a climbing wall and birthday parties are a part of the programs available to keep kids in shape. **Ages: All. Fee.**

The Kiln, 6421 N.W. Cosby Ave., Kansas City, MO 64151, 816-746-4222. Kids can make their own dry-erase boards, drawer pulls or light switch covers for their rooms, as well as gift items for others. This Kiln hosts birthday parties and summer creative workshops. **Ages: 5 and up. Fee.**

TWA Museum, 11730 N. Ambassador Dr., Kansas City, MO 64153, 816-741-1391. Located in the KCI Expo Center, this collection of memorabilia from more than 75 years of Trans World Airlines history fills display cases along the corridors and in the café. Children particularly like the model airplanes and old flight simulators. Guided tours are available by appointment. **Ages: All. Free for children.**

United Federation of Doll Clubs Museum, 10900 N. Pomona Ave., Kansas City, MO 64153, 816-891-7040, www.ufdc.org**.** This delightful museum is home to a collection of more than 700 dolls dating from the 1700s to today. The gift shop has a wonderful collection of unusual dolls for sale. Check the website for special events that include American Girl tea parties. **Ages: All. Fee.**

TRIVIA

BLANCHE BARROW, WHO WAS THE SISTER-IN-LAW OF CLYDE BARROW OF BONNIE AND CLYDE FAME, WAS TRIED AND CONVICTED AT THE PLATTE COUNTY COURTHOUSE IN PLATTE CITY IN 1933. SHE WAS CAPTURED AFTER A JULY 19, 1933 SHOOT-OUT BETWEEN THE BARROW GANG AND PLATTE COUNTY SHERIFF'S DEPARTMENT MEMBERS ON THE GROUNDS OF WHAT IS NOW KANSAS CITY INTERNATIONAL AIRPORT. CLYDE'S BROTHER BUCK WAS KILLED IN THE SHOOT-OUT, AND THREE LAWMEN WERE WOUNDED.

FUN FOOD AND TREATS

Bill's Frozen Custard, 6407 N. Cosby Dr., Kansas City, MO 64151, 816-741-5280. Enjoy your locally-made custard on an outdoor patio while watching the kittens play in the neighboring rock wall.

LC's Hamburgers, 7612 N.W. Prairie View Rd., Kansas City, MO 64151, 816-741-6027. Just five little tables with four little stools are all there is to this 50-year-old burger joint that has people lined up out the door from open to close.

Stone Canyon Pizza, 15 Main St., Parkville, MO 64152, 816-746-8686, www.stonecanyonpizza.com**.** In addition to one of the best gourmet pizza offerings in town, Stone Canyon provides a clown and magician to entertain kids on Friday and Saturday nights.

SHOPPING

Noggin Noodle, 8624 N. Boardwalk Blvd., Kansas City, MO 64154, 816-587-7200. All of the employees at this specialty store are trained educators who appreciate the value of educational toys. The shop hosts weekly craft classes for children ages 2-6 to explore their creativity.

H.M.S. Beagle, 180 English Landing Dr., Parkville, MO 64152, 816-587-9998, www.hms-beagle.com**.** Part museum, part retail center, this educational center invites kids to explore the remains of Polly, a 125 million year old dinosaur, as well as other fossils, rocks and treasures in the store. Come in weekly for tip sheets on the "Mineral of the Week." And while you're there, check out the telescopes, microscopes and other science kits.

PLATTE CITY, WESTON, AND BEYOND

WELCOME

Weston Development Company, 502 Main St., Weston, MO 64098, 816-640-2909, www.westonmo.com. The city's webpage has a coloring book you can print off at home for the kids to color before their visit to town.

COMMUNITY CENTERS

Platte County North Community Center, 3101 Running Horse Rd., Platte City, MO 64079, 816-858-0114. New to the community in the fall of 2004, this center includes an indoor pool and outdoor water park, along with indoor and outdoor playgrounds, and a gymnasium. Ask about the "romp and stomp" program that allows kids to burn off energy indoors on rainy or snowy days.

THE GREAT OUTDOORS

Weston Bend State Park, Weston, MO 64098, 816-640-5443, www.mostateparks.com/westonbend.htm**.** A three-mile paved walking path leads to spectacular view of the Missouri River. Look for the historic markers that detail the Lewis and Clark Expedition through this region. Picnic sites, camping and playgrounds are a part of this 1,100-acre park, which is a trail head for the Weston Bluff Trail, a 3.2 mile paved trail that follows Highway 92 into downtown Weston.

THINGS TO DO

Allredge Orchards, 10455 Hwy. N., Platte City, MO 64079, 816-330-3448. This fun U-pick location has apples, peaches and pumpkins, as well as a country store and bakery. Take a hayride in the autumn months. **Ages: All. Fee.**

Basswood Country Resort, 15880 Interurban Rd., Platte City, MO 64079, 816-858-5556, www.basswoodresort.com. Spend the night camping in the great outdoors, or just come for a day of fishing, swimming, horseshoes and other relaxing activities. Equipment rental and day rates available. **Ages: All. Fee.**

Ben Ferrel Platte County Museum, 220 Ferrel St., Platte City, MO 64079, 816-431-5121. If this building looks familiar, that's because it is an 1881 replica of the Missouri Governor's Mansion in Jefferson City. County historical archives are here and furnishings are to period. **Ages: All. Fee.**

Comanche Acres Iris Gardens, 12421 S.E. Hwy. 116, Gower, MO 64454, 816-424-6436, www.comancheacres.com. This 17-acre garden is most beautiful in the month of May, but is open all year for visit. Kids enjoy the peacocks, rabbits and guinea hens that roam the grounds. **Ages: All. Fee for purchases.**

Herbert Bonnell Museum, 20755 Lamar Rd., Weston, MO 64098, 816-992-0102. This 1874 working farm has the original furnishings and outbuildings. Kids will enjoy the huge arrowhead. Bring a picnic lunch to eat outdoors by the waterfall on the property. **Ages: All. Fee.**

Pumpkins Etc., Farmers Lane, Platte City, MO 64079, 816-858-5758. This family-owned farm four miles east of Platte City on Hwy. 92 opens up the old barn each autumn for the sale of pumpkins from their U-pick pumpkin patch. There are straw-bale mazes built for the five year-old and haystacks to jump in. Tours by appointment. **Ages: All. Free.**

Shiloh Springs Golf Course, 14750 Fairway Ln., Platte City, MO 64079, 816-270-4653, www.shilohspringsgolf.com. This 18-hole course, set in the rolling hills of Platte County, offers an extensive junior program and summer camp for kids. **Ages: 7-17. Fee.**

Snow Creek Ski Area, Weston, MO 64098, 816-640-2200, www.skisnowcreek.com. Metropolitan Kansas City's only downhill ski course, Snow Creek has man-made snow, two beginner and nine intermediate runs, rope tows, snow-boarding hills and lessons. **Ages: 2 and up. Fee.**

Vaughn Orchard and Country Store, 23200 Hwy. 273, Weston, MO 64098, 816-386-2900. Educational tours and hayrides are available through this family farm where apples and pumpkins and their by-products are popular items at the country store. **Ages: All. Fee.**

Weston Red Barn Farm, 16300 Wilkerson Rd., Weston, MO 64098, 816-386-5437, www.westonredbarnfarm.com. Pick your own crops on a seasonal basis, wander through a milo maze or take a hayride, pet the draft horses or feed the baby goats. Educational tours are available, but families can spend hours just enjoying the scenic beauty of rural Platte County from this location. **Ages: All. Fee for purchases.**

Wild Rose Equine Center, 17105 Old Pike Rd., Dearborn, MO 64439, 816-450-8636. In addition to trailrides for the family or a group of friends, this center provides lessons in western and English style riding. On the grounds, there is a picnic area and an open pit grill. **Age: 8 and up. Fee.**

WORRIED ABOUT YOUR TEENAGERS DRINKING? VISIT WWW.THECOOLSPOT.GOV. BETTER YET, BOOKMARK THE SITE FOR THEM OR SEND THEM LITTLE TIDBITS OF INFORMATION FOUND ON THIS GOVERNMENT SPONSORED WEBSITE.

LEAVENWORTH COUNTY, KS

INCLUDES LANSING, LEAVENWORTH, FORT LEAVENWORTH

WELCOME

Leavenworth/Lansing Convention and Visitors Bureau, 518 Shawnee St., Leavenworth, KS 66048, 913-682-4113, www.lvarea.com.

THE GREAT OUTDOORS

Lansing Parks and Recreation Department, 108 South Second St., Lansing, KS 913-727-2960. Fishing derbies, soccer, basketball, T-ball and other events are coordinated from the offices in the Activity Center, where an open gym is available to the public.

Leavenworth Parks and Recreation Department, 123 S. Esplanade, Leavenworth, KS 66048, 913-651-2132, www.lvks.org. This city department operates numerous recreational leagues and coordinates special events throughout the year.

COMMUNITY CENTERS

Riverfront Community Center, 123 S. Esplanade, Leavenworth, KS, 66048, 913-651-2132. This former train station from the 1850s is worth exploration itself for the fabulous architecture and history of the city. But kids will like the indoor pool and the numerous recreational events held here.

AREA PARKS AND PLAYGROUNDS

Buffalo Bill Cody Park, Shrine Park & Limit, Leavenworth. This pleasant park has lots of playground equipment, restrooms, lighted tennis courts, a baseball field, and walking trail.

Dougherty Park, 2nd & Kiowa, Leavenworth. This pleasantly shaded park is located by the Missouri River with lots of playground equipment, picnic tables and restrooms.

Leavenworth Landing, Esplanade & Cherokee, downtown Leavenworth. Teach local geography to children through the brass four-state map in this riverfront park that includes rivers, trails and railroads that were an important part of Kansas history. You'll also find markers commemorating the Lewis and Clark Expedition in this area.

Wollman Park, 13th and Shawnee, Leavenworth. New to the city in 2003 is the aquatic center in this park, which includes slides, a kiddie pool and sprayground, diving pool and zero-depth entry.

THINGS TO DO

Carroll Mansion, 1128 Fifth Avenue, Leavenworth, KS 66048, 913-682-7759 or 800-844-4114. This 1882 Victorian home is both a museum to that era and the site of numerous activities for children that introduce them to that genteel period of history. Kids love the tour of the home when they end up in the child's room filled with antique toys. **Ages: Fee.**

C.W. Parker Carousel Museum, 320 S. Esplanade St., Leavenworth, KS 66048, 913-682-1866. What child doesn't love old-fashioned carousels? This museum salutes the work of the C.W. Parker Amusement Company that operated in Leavenworth prior to the Great Depression. You will be able to ride on a 1913 C.W. Parker Carousel that has been restored. The carousel has 24 hand-carved horses, three ponies and a lover's cup to ride in. Another carousel features flying horses. **Ages: All. Free.**

Doolittle Farms, 28013 167th St., Leavenworth, KS 66048, 913-772-6971, www.doolittlefarms.com**.** This 80-acre retreat has fishing lakes, hiking trails, and scheduled hayrides, as well as primitive camping and log-cabins for rent. The farm is the site of several educational classes about the environment and farm life and hosts special events such as the High Prairie Jamboree, a blue grass festival each June. The gift shop is great for home-grown farm products. **Ages: All. Fee.**

Fort Leavenworth, 913-684-5604. Established in 1827, this is the oldest army fort in continuous operation west of the Mississippi River. Some of the more legendary names in American history have been associated with Fort Leavenworth – George Custer, Robert E. Lee, Douglas McArthur, George Patton, Colin Powell. The fort is a community unto itself and provides insight into the life of the United States military. **NOTE: Picture ID's are required of all adults ages 16 and over upon entering the Fort.**

Berlin Wall Monument - Three sections of the Berlin Wall were donated to Fort Leavenworth after the barrier to freedom came down in 1989.

Buffalo Soldiers Memorial – This monument opens discussion with children about a time when the armed services were segregated and these African-American soldiers, called Buffalo Soldier by the Cheyenne, served with honor from 1866 until the end of World War II. It's location by Smith Lake is a great place for a picnic lunch. Often there are many ducks to feed by the lake.

Frontier Army Museum, 913-684-3767 – The exhibits here tell the history of the U.S. Army and its role in western expansion of the United States. A special story hour about pioneer life is offered to elementary school children by appointment.

Lansing Historical Museum, 115 E. Kansas Ave., Lansing, KS 66043, 913-250-0203. Located in a restored 1887 Santa Fe Depot adjacent to the Lansing Correctional Facility this museum has lots of railroad memorabilia, including a telegrapher's room. There are also exhibits from Lansing's early days, as well as a special exhibit on the history of the prisons in the region. **Ages:10 and up. Free.**

Richard Allen Cultural Center, 412 Kiowa, Leavenworth, KS 66048, 913-682-8772. This museum offers a glimpse into the history of African-Americans locally and nationwide with numerous displays including sections on General Colin Powell, Buffalo Soldiers and a sports section. **Ages: All. Fee.**

FUN FOOD AND TREATS

The Corner Pharmacy, 429 Delaware St., Leavenworth, KS 66048, 913-682-1602. Kids have enjoyed ice cream and other treats on the round-swivel stools at this soda fountain since 1871. In addition to breakfast and lunch, stop in for hand made shakes, malts and fresh-squeezed lemonade.

Homer's Drive In, 1320 S. Fourth St., Leavenworth, KS 66048, 913-651-3034. You can still get a frosty mug of root beer and a great cheeseburger at this family-friendly joint that's been serving up good times since 1931.

TRIVIA

YOU'LL SEE BUFFALO BILL CODY'S NAME THROUGHOUT THE LEAVENWORTH AREA. HE MOVED HERE WHEN HE WAS EIGHT AND WORKED FOR THE OVERLAND STAGE LINE IN LEAVENWORTH. AN ORGANIZED BIKE RIDE EACH SEPTEMBER TOURS SEVERAL OF THE PLACES ASSOCIATED WITH BUFFALO BILL'S PRESENCE IN THE AREA. CALL 913-682-8918 OR VISIT WWW.LVNBICYCLE.VZE.COM FOR MORE INFORMATION.

WYANDOTTE COUNTY, KS

KANSAS CITY, BONNER SPRINGS, EDWARDSVILLE

WELCOME

Kansas Travel Information Center, exit 410 off of I-70, 913-299-2253. You'll find brochures and lots of information about sites throughout Kansas here, as well as free coffee and modern restrooms. The Kansas Speedway Pit Shop is also located here where, in addition to racing memorabilia, you can buy products made in Kansas.

Kansas City, Kansas/Wyandotte County Convention and Visitors Bureau, 727 Minnesota, Kansas City, KS 66101, 913-321-5800, www.kckcvb.org**.**

KANSAS CITY KANSAS

ASSISTANCE

Huggers (Special Olympics) Hot Line, 913-406-6003

Kaw Valley Arts & Humanities, 155 S. 18th St., Kansas City, KS 66117, 913-371-0024, www.artsnoboundaries.org**.** Children of Wyandotte County receive access to traditional arts brought to this country by immigrants of old through this non-profit organization,

Kaw Valley Center, 4300 Brenner Dr., Kansas City, KS 66104, 913-334-0294, www.kawvalley.org**.** This non-profit organization provides a number of mental health and family counseling services for families with children up to 21 years of age. For high school juniors in Wyandotte County, the Leadership 2020 program provides awareness of community issues, such as education, government, social services, media, careers and economics.

K-State Research and Extension, 9400 State Ave., Kansas City, KS 66112, 913-299-9300, www.oznet.ksu.edu/wyandotte/. This is where you can get your kids involved in 4-H and other programs that provide information on leadership, safety and nutrition.

COMMUNITY CENTERS

Argentine Community Center, 2810 Metropolitan Ave., Kansas City, KS, 913-261-4382.

Armourdale Recreation Center, 930 Osage, Kansas City, KS, 913-551-0408.

Bethany Community Center, 1120 Central Ave., Kansas City, KS, 913-551-0400.

Eisenhower Recreation Center, 2901 N. 72nd St., Kansas City, KS, 913-596-7050.

George Meyn Building, 126th & State Ave., in Wyandotte County Park, 913-596-7050.

Kensington Recreation Center, 2900 State Ave., Kansas City, KS 913-551-0406

THE GREAT OUTDOORS

Unified Government Parks and Recreation, Youth Information Office, 5033 State Ave., Kansas City, KS 66102, 913-573-8330 or 913-596-7077, www.wycokc.org/departments/.

SPECIAL AREA PARKS AND PLAYGROUNDS

Kaw Point, 1 River City Dr., Kansas City, KS. Renovated to coincide with the bicentennial of the Lewis and Clark Expedition, this six acre park features an open-air education pavilion with interpretive signs about the expedition as well as an interactive computer element. Trails run through the woods and along the river. A boat ramp allows access to the Missouri River, which merges with the Kansas River, sometimes called the Kaw River, at this point.

Kansas City Kansas Community College Nature Trail, 7250 State Ave., Kansas City, KS 66112, 913-288-7358. The two-mile trail is marked with signs identifying trees, plants and other flora. Aside from holding the largest Burr Oak in Kansas, the trail is an excellent place for birding and seeing small mammals. Trail guide are available from the college fieldhouse or science division. Open all year, the trail is particularly beautiful after a snow.

Rosedale Park, 41st and Mission, Kansas City, KS. The highlights of this 55-acre park include a frisbee golf course, a skateboard park and a modern playground.

Pierson Park, 1800 S. 55th St., Kansas City, KS. A sprayground was added to this popular park in 2004. There's also a fishing lake, tennis courts, two playgrounds and nice picnic areas.

Wyandotte County Lake Park, 91st and Leavenworth Rd., Kansas City, KS. There's something of interest for everyone here, including boat rentals, a playground and a fishing pond reserved exclusively for children. No fishing license is needed for those under 16 years old. There's also a model train for kids to ride the second Saturday of each month. Bring the family out here for a pleasant drive around the lake to see wildlife and water fowl, or to take a minute paying tribute at the Korean and Vietnam Veterans Memorial at the park's entrance.

THINGS TO DO

Argentine Wall, 30th and Metropolitan, Kansas City, KS. Teach kids about the people who have settled in this area from Argentina. The mural is 220 yards long and nearly 30 feet high in some places and documents the life and times of the residents of the Argentine area of Kansas City. A brochure, available at the KCK Convention and Visitors Bureau (913-321-5800), helps interpret the panels.

Children's Museum of Kansas City, 4601 State Ave., Kansas City, KS 66102, 913-287-8888, www.kidmuzm.org**.** This is a place where you don't have to worry about the kids touching things. They are encouraged to do so in the many interactive exhibits that explore everything from electricity to careers and the natural environment. After-school programs are tailored for scouting badge requirements. A "Classroom on Wheels" is also available to bring a fossil dig to your school that includes a replica dinosaur skeleton. The museum is a great place to celebrate a birthday as well. **Ages: 2-9. Fee.**

Donnelly College, 608 N. 18th St., Kansas City, KS 66102, 913-621-6070. Donnelly College is home to the Roe Collection, an historical record of African Americans in this region that includes artwork, relics, documents, photos and clothing. **Ages: 9 and up. Free.**

General Motors Plant, 3201 Fairfax Trafficway, Kansas City, KS 66115, 913-573-7643. Watch how the Chevy Malibu and other General Motors vehicles are made during this two-hour tour that covers all aspects of auto assembling and finishing. Kids will love the robot assembly area. Tours must be arranged in advance, usually about a month's notice. **Ages: 12 and up. Free.**

Great Wolf Lodge, 10401 Cabela Dr., Kansas City, KS 66111, 913-299-7001, www.greatwolflodge.com**.** This is a vacation destination in itself with enough to do to keep the whole family happy for days. The four-story log resort is highlighted by a 38,000 square-foot water park that moves from indoors to out and is open all year for guests of the lodge. The indoor part is called Bear Track Landing and includes eight waterslides, five pools, and two whirlpools. The outdoor area is called Thunder Bay, which includes treehouses, water basketball and 12 levels of water-based adventure connected through suspension bridges and cargo nets.

In addition, there's a 6,000 square foot arcade, a children's activity area, board games in the lobby and guest rooms that feel like you're spending the night in a log cabin in the Northwoods of Minnesota. There's a children's story time by the fireplace every night.

Even if you're not spending the night, visit the lobby to see the animated clock tower with a singing moose, owl and turtle. Authentic totem poles reflect the culture of the North American tribes of Haida, Tsimshian and Tlinget. **Ages: All. Fee.**

Grinter State Historical Site, 1420 S. 78th St., Kansas City, KS 66111, 913-299-0373. This is the home of Moses and Anna Grinter, who were among the earliest pioneers in Kansas. They established the first ferry crossing across the Kansas River near here. The house is considered the oldest farmhouse in the state and includes furnishings from the late 19th century. **Ages: 5 and up. Fee.**

Huron Indian Cemetery, 7th and Ann St., Kansas City, KS 66101, 913-721-1078. This cemetery was established in 1843 after the forced migration of the Wyandot Nation from their lands in Ohio. It is adjacent to the Kansas City Kansas Public Library, where you can read more about the work to save the cemetery by the Conley sisters, members of the Wyandot Nation. **Ages: All. Free.**

Kansas Speedway, I-70 and I-435, 913-328-7223, www.kansasspeedway.com**.** This 1.5 mile tri-oval race track feature many exciting races, including NASCAR Nextel events. The speedway offers a kid's club that includes a tour of Victory Lane, the spotter's stand, the garages and more. You'll also get a birthday card from the mascot Victor E. Lane. For specific information on kid's club membership, call 913-328-3300. **Ages: All. Fee.**

Lakeside Speedway, 5615 Wolcott Dr., Kansas City, KS 66109, 913-299-2040, www.inthepits.net**.** This half-mile dirt oval track, which has been entertaining Kansas City area families for 50 years, is part of the NASCAR Weekly Racing Series. Racing is held Friday nights, March through September. **Ages: All. Kids under seven get in free.**

Outdoor Fishing Derby, 913-788-3988. Several governmental agencies combine to hold numerous half-day fishing clinics for Wyandotte County children in the warm weather months. The program teaches about fishing and sportsmanship, while awarding prizes for the biggest and smallest catch. **Ages: 16 and under. Free.**

Parkwood Pool, 950 Quindaro, Kansas City, KS, 913-551-0402. This traditional city pool includes a wading pool, slides and a diving area. **Ages: All. Fee.**

Strawberry Hill Museum and Cultural Center, 720 N. 4th St., Kansas City, KS 66101, 913-371-3264, www.heritageleaguekc.org/strawberryhill/**.** Located in a Queen Anne-style home built in 1887, this museum preserves the diverse ethnic cultures that immigrants from Eastern Europe brought to Kansas City in the early 1900s. There's a tearoom open on weekends. **Ages: All. Fee, those under 6 are free.**

Thunderlake Speedway, 5501 Wolcott Dr., Kansas City, KS 66109, 913-299-2323 or 913-334-5766, www.thunderlakespeedway.com**.** This is the place to come to race go-carts! This is a 1/5-mile oval dirt track where races are held on Saturdays from April through November. **Ages: 5 and up. Fee.**

Kansas City T-Bones Baseball, 1800 Village West Parkway, Kansas City, KS 66111, 913-328-BALL (2255), www.tbonesbaseball.com**.** A kids play area in right field and the crazy antics of Sizzle the mascot make a night at this family-friendly ballpark a low-stress family experience. A specially-designed concession stand with lower counters and lower prices makes kids feel at home. Wednesday nights are Family Night. **Ages: All. Fee.**

Unified Government of Kansas City Kansas, 701 N. 7th St., Kansas City, KS 66101, 913-573-5469, www.wycokck.org**.** This tour covers two buildings, which includes the courts, the police departments I.D. unit, line-up and communication rooms. Kids may enjoy the aerial mapping unit where they will be able to see their home on a large wall display in the courthouse. The volunteer office coordinates the 45-minute tour that can be tailored to your group's needs and interests. **Ages: 10 and up. Free.**

FUN FOOD AND TREATS

Franklin Center, 1400 Metropolitan, Kansas City, KS 63103, 913-342-9248, www.franklincenter.org**.** The school building from the 1900s has been turned into a community action center, including a restaurant where meals are wholesome and inexpensive. Kids will enjoy huge ice cream sundaes for about $1.50. Check out the menu on-line before visiting.

Fritz's Restaurant, 250 N. 18th St., Kansas City, KS 66102, 913-281-2777. A fun restaurant to take young and old railroad fans, a burger at this Kansas City tradition is delivered to tables by overhead electric trains. Kids get a paper engineer's hat.

SHOPPING

Cabela's, 10300 Cabela Dr., Kansas City, KS 66111, 913-328-0322, www.cabelas.com**.** Part retail center, part natural science museum, Cabela's is filled with elaborate displays of wildlife from around the world, including bear, antelope and cougars. The Mule Deer Museum displays more than 80 record-class mule deer in a natural setting. Also check out the three aquariums totaling more than 55,000 gallons that contain fish native to lakes and rivers in Kansas and Missouri. If you like, the kids may shoot a bow and arrow in the archery range or shoot a laser gun at the African exhibit. Guided tours are available that explain the animals and where they are from.

BONNER SPRINGS AND EDWARDSVILLE

WELCOME

Bonner Springs/Edwardsville Chamber of Commerce, PO Box 403, Bonner Springs, KS 66012, 913-422-5044, www.bonnersprings.org. A Visitor Information Center is located in the caboose in Centennial Park, 126 Cedar St.

THE GREAT OUTDOORS

Bonner Springs Parks and Recreation, 200 E. Third, Bonner Springs, KS 66012, 913-422-7010 or 913-422-5877. The city coordinates a swim team, a baseball league and a city band, among other programs.

Kerry Roberts Park, K-7 and Kansas Ave., Bonner Springs. This park, in memory of a boy who was fatally injured during a baseball game, serves as a nature park with a shelter house in the back portion of the park, picnic tables with grills, and playground equipment.

Wyandotte County Park, 126th and State Ave., Bonner Springs, KS 66102, 913-596-7077. Frisbee golf and a skateboard park are among the fun things to do in this park adjacent to the Sunflower Hills Golf Course. A large children's playground, a junior golf course and a six-acre fishing lake are additional amenities.

THINGS TO DO

Agricultural Hall of Fame, 630 Hall of Fame Dr., Bonner Springs, KS 66012, 913-721-1075, www.aghalloffame.com. This extensive facility tells the history of agriculture and its innovations that have helped make the United States the most powerful country in the world. In addition to seeing more than 30,000 agricultural artifacts, including Harry Truman's plow, your children will enjoy a trip through Farm Town and a ride on the authentic narrow-gauge railroad built by Union Pacific employees. There's a nature trail and lots of picnic areas. Watch the website for special events throughout the year that allow kids to become farmers for a day. **Ages: 3 and up. Fee.**

Moon Marble Company, 600 E. Front St., Bonner Springs, KS 66012, 913-441-1432, www.moonmarble.com. This is such a fun wholesome place for families! Watch as marbles are being made and get down on the floor to learn the old-fashioned game of marbles. The website has downloadable marble games. **Ages: 4 and up. Fee for purchases.**

Wyandotte County Museum, 631 N. 126th St., Bonner Springs, KS 66012, 913-721-1078. This is the perfect museum to take kids to learn about the early days of Kansas history and the American Indians who made their home here. Exhibits include a dug-out canoe, arrowheads and other artifacts, and information on the Lewis and Clark Expedition. More modern exhibits include a horse-drawn fire engine and a B-25 tail stabilizer that was built in Wyandotte County during World War II. Outside are an heirloom garden and a fountain recognizing the work of the Humane Society. **Ages: All. Fee.**

FUN FOOD AND TREATS

Simple Simon's Pizza, 11647 Kaw Dr., Bonner Springs, KS 66012, 913-441-6764. Kids say the game room at this locally-owned establishment is the best in the area. Parents will appreciate that the restaurant is non-smoking and no alcohol is served here.

TRIVIA

INTERSTATE 635, THAT RUNS THROUGH EASTERN WYANDOTTE COUNTY, IS DEDICATED TO HARRY DARBY, A U. S. SENATOR FROM KANSAS WHO WAS BORN IN WYANDOTTE COUNTY. HE WAS CHAIRMAN OF THE STATE HIGHWAY COMMISSION FROM 1933-1937.

JOHNSON COUNTY, KS

INCLUDES OVERLAND PARK, LEAWOOD, FAIRWAY, PRAIRIE VILLAGE, SHAWNEE, MERRIAM, LENEXA, OLATHE, LOUISBURG, STILWELL, GARDNER AND EDGERTON

TRANSPORTATION

Johnson County Transit, 913-541-8450, www.thejo.com. Allow your children to experience the value of public transit and fuel conservation. Take The Jo! The buses are equipped with bicycle racks, so you can ride the bus to your favorite park to ride your bike.

ASSISTANCE

Day Care Connection, 8855 Long, Lenexa, KS 66215, 913-529-1200, www.daycareconnection.org. This referral agency represents more than 1,000 homes and facilities offering day care in Johnson County and provides training and support to employees of day care facilities.

Healthy Kids University, 816-234-3748. Coordinated through Children's Mercy Hospital South, these programs are offered at your request and designed to meet the needs of your group on any health or safety topic.

Homework Help is available for Johnson County students in grade four to eight at the Central Resource Library, 9875 W. 87th St., Overland Park, after school and on Sundays. Call 913-261-2300.

Johnson County Parents Association, 913-696-9771. This support group of parents with pre-school aged kids is geared toward the whole family and offers playgroups throughout the week and family activities at night and on weekends.

Kansas City Children's Assistance Network, 5340 College Blvd., Overland Park, KS 66211, 913-696-0500, www.kccan.org. Among its public service projects for Kansas City kids is to help provide safe, high quality playgrounds to targeted areas in Kansas City that have unsafe playgrounds or no playground at all.

Midwest Wholechild Development Group, 8001 Conser, # 280, Overland Park, KS 66204, 913-341-6200, www.mwdg.org. This non-profit association provides child care referral services for Johnson and Miami County residents and employees.

Mothers and More of Greater Johnson County, 913-451-7784, www.jocomothersandmore.com. The meetings of this support group are held at the Grace Covenant Presbyterian Church, 11100 College Blvd. the first and third Tuesday of the month.

The Great Outdoors

Johnson County Parks and Recreation, 6501 Antioch, Merriam, KS 66202, 913-831-3355, www.jcprd.com. The services, classes, programs and educational activities offered through Johnson County Parks and Recreation are all but endless. Call for the quarterly catalogue of seasonal activities or visit the department's extensive on-line website.

The Streamway Park System. Crisscrossing more than 170 miles in Johnson County, this park system is comprised of paved walking and biking trails that follow the path of eight major streams in Johnson County. This includes Mill Creek, Kill Creek, Indian Creek, Tomahawk Creek, and more. The park is managed cooperatively by the municipalities through which the trails cross. This initiative is a part of the Metro Green program coordinated by the Mid America Regional Council (www.marc.org/metrogreen).

Worried about your teenagers drinking? Visit www.thecoolspot.gov. Better yet, bookmark the spot for them or send them little reminders available on the website.

OVERLAND PARK, LEAWOOD

WELCOME

Overland Park Convention and Visitors Bureau, 9001 W. 110th St., # 100, Overland Park, KS 66210, 913-491-0123, www.opcvb.org**.**

Leawood Chamber of Commerce, 11250 Tomahawk Creek Pkwy., Leawood, KS 66211, 913-498-1514, www.leawoodchamber.org**.**

COMMUNITY CENTERS

Carlson Cultural Education Center, Johnson County Community College, 12345 College Blvd., Overland Park, KS 66212, 913-469-8500, www.jccc.net**.** Three theatres at this center host numerous performances for families of all interests. The art gallery offers program for all ages, as well as other programs at the center designed to meet the interests of the diverse Johnson County population.

Leawood Community Center, 4800 Town Center Blvd., Leawood, KS 66211, 913-339-6700, ext. 201. Located in the lower level of city hall, this center has four meeting rooms for parties, clubs and groups.

Overland Park Community Center, 6300 W. 87th St., Overland Park, KS 66212, 913-895-6390. Summer programs galore, as well as seasonal workshops for kids, and activities such as Easter egg hunts and Halloween parties, are coordinated here through Johnson County Parks and Recreation.

Overland Park International Trade Center, 6800 W. 115th St., Overland Park, KS 66211, 913-451-6124, www.opitc.com**.** This center is filled with numerous public activities and events throughout the year, many of them appropriate for families with children. Call the information line to find out what may be happening today.

ASSISTANCE

El Centro Family Resource Center, 9525 Metcalf Ave., Overland Park, KS 66212, 913-381-2861. This non-profit organization provides tutoring for children of Hispanic origins and emergency assistance for families in crisis.

Parent Resource Center, 6601 Santa Fe Dr., Shawnee Mission, KS 66202, 913-993-9315. Located in the Arrowhead Administration Center of the Shawnee Mission School District, this program offers help on a number of parenting issues, such as discipline, study skills and socialization. There's a lending library of tapes and videos, as well as classes for parents on many subjects.

THE GREAT OUTDOORS

Deanna Rose Memorial Farmstead, 138th and Switzer, Overland Park, KS 66221, 913-897-2360, www.deannarosefarmstead.org**.** Designed to depict an early 20th-century Kansas farm, this eight-acre educational center includes a petting zoo, a silo with slides, a tot-lot for the younger children, a farmhouse and gardens. Kids especially enjoy feeding the baby goats in the spring. Wagon rides are available. Gardening demonstrations are common. **Ages: All. Fee**.

Ironwoods Park, 147th and Mission Rd., Leawood. This 50-acre park was new to the city in 2004 and includes a playground, amphitheatre, nature center, and challenge course with a rock climbing wall and tree houses. The Leawood Historic Commission relocated the Oxford School here, an 1877 one-room school house, complete with outhouse. Programs are held here throughout the year, including ice cream socials and lectures. The park also has four cabins for rent and a fire ring appropriate for scouting programs.

PASSIVE ACTIVITIES, SUCH AS WATCHING TV, DEPRIVE A CHILD'S BRAIN OF SENSORY, HANDS-ON ACTIVITIES THAT SIMULATE BRAIN GROWTH. SOURCE: WWW.KCBRAINCHILD.ORG

Leawood City Park and Pool, 10601 Lee Blvd., Leawood, KS 66211, 913-327-3977. The pools here include a baby pool with slides, a zero-depth entry pool with waterfalls and a floating lizard, and another lap pool with a giant whale. Swim lessons are offered. The park also has a pond and two age-specific playgrounds, as well as 12 soccer fields, tennis courts and a walking trail.

Thomas S. Stoll Memorial Park, 12500 W. 119th St., Overland Park. This 79-acre park includes seven athletic fields, a small fishing lake, picnic shelters, playgrounds, a walking trail and an off-leash dog area.

Overland Park Arboretum and Botanical Gardens, 8909 W. 179th St., Overland Park, KS 66225, 913-685-3604, www.overlandparkarboretum.org. This 300-acre park has nine miles of woodchip and sidewalk trail perfect for pushing strollers through numerous garden areas. The Environmental Education Center has rotating exhibits on animals and insects, which kids should find interesting. **Ages: All. Free.**

THINGS TO DO

All Fired Up, 7915 Santa Fe Dr., Overland Park, KS 66204, 913-385-5456, www.justglazeit.com. This paint-your-own pottery store is a great place to stir a child's creativity. Scouts can earn a pottery badge with a tour of the studio. **Ages: 5-12. Fee.**

AMF Ranchmart Bowling Lanes and Ice Chateau, 8788 Metcalf, Overland Park, KS 66212, 913-648-2100 or 913-648-0129 (ice rink). The upstairs of this facility is an expansive bowling alley and video arcade, which includes private birthday party rooms. Downstairs is the ice rink. Children under four must have an adult on the ice with them at all times. **Ages: All. Fee.**

All-Golf Family Recreation Center, 10350 W. 135th St., Overland Park, KS 66221, 913-681-8887. Open all year, this center has two 18-hole miniature golf courses, batting cages, a driving range and an arcade. **Ages: 3 and up. Fee.**

BumpCity/Monster Mountain, 9063 Bond, Overland Park, KS 66214, 913-438-7775. This colorful, indoor playland includes a 12-foot rock climbing wall, slides, swimming ropes that drop you into foam pits and a zip-line overhead. **Ages: 4-12. Fee.**

Gymboree, 7399 W. 97th St., Overland Park, KS 66211, 913-469-1118. A full line-up of classes that include music, art and playtime are designed to meet the growing skills and interests of kids. New challenges and experiences take place each week. Baby-sign language is a new addition to the curriculum. **Ages: Birth to 6. Fee.**

Incred-a-Bowl, 8500 W. 151st St., Overland Park, KS 66223, 913-851-1700, www.incredabowl.com**.** It's not your average bowling alley. In addition to a 10,000 square feet arcade, former Royals player Danny Jackson and his wife have built a 40-lane cosmic bowling alley, a children's play center and a restaurant. This is a great spot for birthday parties. **Ages: All. Fee.**

Manners Classes, 6304 W. 127th Terr., Overland Park, KS 66209, 913-685-4726. Are your kids clods? Have no social graces? Consider a course in etiquette that includes proper introductions, table manners and other elements of etiquette that would make Miss Manners jump for joy. Classes are held separately for boys and girls. **Ages: 6-16. Fee.**

Martin City Melodrama and Vaudeville Co., 9601 Metcalf, Overland Park, KS 66212, 913-642-7576, www.martincitymelodrama.com**.** Since 1985, this dinner theatre has produced traditional melodramas, barbershop quartets, and musicals that offer good clean fun for the entire family. In 2003, the company started Martin City, Jr., a children's theatre. All year classes and summer camps focuses on theatre skills for kids, all located within Metcalf South Shopping Center. **Fee. Ages: 5 and up.**

Midwest Center for Holocaust Education, 5801 W. 115th St., Overland Park, KS 66222, 913-327-8190. The center offers books, videotapes and software to area teachers and anyone interested in learning the story of the Holocaust from Holocaust survivors who make their home in Kansas City. The center sponsors an essay contest on the subject each year for high school students. **Ages: High school only. Free.**

Overland Park Golf Club, 12501 Quivira Rd., Overland Park, KS 66213, 913-897-3809. Children eight and older are welcome to play on the full 18-hole course as well as a 9-hole par 3 course. Junior lessons are available ages 5-17. A three-day tournament each August allows kids 4-17 to demonstrate their skills. **Ages: 4 and up. Fee.**

Paint, Glaze and Fire, 12683 Metcalf, Overland Park, KS 66213, 913-661-2529, www.paintglazeandfire.com. Little girls will enjoy making their own child-sized tea set here while learning about British high tea ceremonies. That's one of several different themes for birthday parties and summer camps. **Ages: 6 and up. Fee.**

Pepsi Ice Midwest & Fitness Center, 12140 W. 135th St., Overland Park, KS 66221, 913-851-1600 or 913-851-1862, www.icemidwest.com. With two full-size ice rinks, a fitness and dance center, game and party rooms, this massive facility is busy all the time with summer day camp, skating classes and competitions, ice hockey tournaments, curling demonstrations and more. Even if you don't get on the ice, it's a great place to visit with the kids. Skating lessons begin at age 3. **Ages: 3 and up. Fee.**

Police Station Tours, 12400 Foster, Overland Park, KS 66221, 913-895-6106. Tours of the police station are offered Tuesday, Wednesday and Thursday afternoons by appointment only offering kids an insight into the work of the Overland Park police and life behind bars. **Ages: 6 and up. Free.**

Skate City, 10440 Mastin, Overland Park, KS 66212, 913-888-6668. A great place for birthday parties or a good time with friends. This family-owned facility includes video games, a snack bar and a modern plastic floor that softens the blow on falls. The center is available for private parties. Saturday mornings are reserved for skaters 12 and under. Roller hockey leagues are also offered here. **Ages: Preschool and up. Fee.**

FUN FOOD AND TREATS

Blue Chip Cookies, 5045 W. 117th St., Leawood, KS 66211, 913-696-1250. This family-owned business makes about 20 flavors of cookies fresh from scratch every day. Kids like the sugar cookies decorated for the season with Blue Bell Ice Cream on top.

Dick Clark's American Bandstand Grill, 10975 Metcalf Ave., Overland Park, KS 66282, 913-451-1600. Drive your kids nuts as you sing the oldies and enjoy the rock n' roll memorabilia from generations past. Consider it a history lesson in this fun restaurant owned by America's oldest teenager.

Rainforest Café, Oak Park Mall, 11327 W. 95th St., Overland Park, KS 66201, 913-438-7676, www.rainforestcafe.com**.** OK. Don't expect the kids to sit still to eat their meal at this wild place. There's so much going on, from monkeys swinging by their tails from the trees overhead to volcanoes blowing to herds of elephants stampeding. No other place in Kansas City offers as much entertainment, and good food as well.

Say Cheese, Oak Park Mall, 11327 W. 95th St., Overland Park, KS 66201, 913-307-2020. If your kids like grilled cheese sandwiches, this is the place to come because they have dozens of variations, along with mac and cheese and other cheesy treats.

Special Shops

Build-A-Bear, 11465 W. 95th St, Overland Park, KS 66214, 913-307-0328 www.buildabear.com**.** Located in Oak Park Mall, this fun place allows you to dress and stuff your own teddy bear or any of about 25 kinds of animals, creating a lovable gift unique to each child. It's a great place for birthday parties. Check the website for some fun on-line activities. **Ages: 4 and up. Fee.**

The Learning Tree, 4816 W. 119th St., Leawood, KS 66211, 913-498-1234, www.toysandgifts.com**.** Not your typical toy store, you'll find lots of stuff to stimulate a child's curiosity and creativity in the shop with hands-on ownership by the parents of three little ones. Check the website for lots of activities, including artist and author visits, story and playtime.

Shear Madness, 6311 W. 119th St. Overland Park, KS 66209, 913-338-4747. Sometimes getting little ones to sit still for a haircut is next to impossible. Here, kids have their own little car and watch television and other videos to entertain them while the snipping takes place. Ask about the Fashion Show Birthday Parties.

FAIRWAY, PRAIRIE VILLAGE, ROELAND PARK

WELCOME

Prairie Village Merchants Association, 3920 W. 69th Terr., Prairie Village, KS 66208, 913-362-9668.

COMMUNITY CENTERS

Roeland Park Community Center, 4850 Rosewood Dr., Roeland Park, KS 66205, 913-722-0039. Most of the programs here are coordinated through Johnson County Park and Recreation (913-831-3355, www.jcprd.com) but family magic shows, Easter celebrations and other special events are coordinated locally throughout the year. Rooms are available for rent for birthday parties, troop meetings and other large gatherings.

Prairie Village Community Center, 7720 Mission Rd., Prairie Village, KS 66205, 913-381-6464, www.pvkansas.com**.** Basic meeting rooms and a kitchen are available for non-profit groups and others for a minimal charge.

THE GREAT OUTDOORS

Fairway City Park and Pool, 61st and Mission, 913-722-3161. This park has two playgrounds with tot swings and age-appropriate climbing apparatus, a sand play area and tennis courts. The pool is one of the few in the metropolitan area with a high dive. There's also a kiddy pool with a slide and a sun deck.

Harmon Park and Aquatic Center, 7711 Delmar, Prairie Village, 913-381-6464. Adjacent to the Prairie Village Municipal building and Community Center, this is the city's premiere park facility and the home of a new skatepark, as well as the city's pool complex, which has two water slides, a plunge pool and zero depth entry. There are lighted tennis courts and lessons available.

THINGS TO DO

Center for Understanding the Built Environment (CUBE), 5328 W. 67th St., Prairie Village, KS 66208, 913-262-8222, www.cubekc.org. This award-winning and unique center brings educators, children and adults together to understand the value of architectural design and planning to build better cities and communities. Curriculum packages bring city design into the classroom, but guided tours of various communities add to the child's understanding of what makes a city livable. **Ages: middle school and up. Fee.**

Gymboree, 3928 W. 69th Terr., Prairie Village, KS 66208, 913-469-1118. A full line-up of classes that include music, art and playtime are designed to meet the growing skills and interests of kids. New challenges and experiences take place each week. Baby-sign language is a new addition to the curriculum. **Ages: Birth to 6. Fee.**

KCTV 5, P.O. Box 5555, Kansas City, MO 64109, 913-677-5555, www.kctv5.com. This CBS affiliate has a speakers' bureau that includes reporters, producers, directors and others who make TV happen. **Ages: 1st grade and up. Free.**

Roeland Park Aquatic Center, 4843 Rosewood, Roeland Park, KS 66205, 913-432-1377. Open year-round with indoor and outdoor pools, this aquatic center has zero-depth entry, fountains, sprayers and slides for the kids, as well as swimming and diving lessons coordinated by Johnson County Parks and Recreation. The outdoor pool has a sandy beach and playground for the kids. **Ages: All. Fee.**

Shawnee Methodist Mission and Indian Manual Labor School, 3403 W. 53rd St., Fairway, KS 66205, 913-262-0867, www.kshs.org. One of the earliest Indian missions established in pre-territorial Kansas (1839), this National Historic Landmark provides insight into the relationship between European white settlers and American Indians during this time period. Kids seem most interested in the furnishings found inside the old-time classroom and dormitories for American Indian children. **Ages: 6 and up. Free.**

FUN FOOD AND TREATS

Laura Little's Candies, 2100 W. 75th St., Prairie Village, KS 66208, 913-722-2226, www.geocities.com/laurasfudge**.** This is the place for delicious fudge, chocolate suckers, caramel apples, popcorn, cookies, cakes and gummy items in shapes of dinosaurs, tarantulas and apes, plus kid-sized ice cream bars. You'll find a nice selection of gift items for kids as well.

Lucy Lynn's Pastry and Party Shop, 5240 Belinder, Fairway, KS 66205, 913-262-2600. This family-owned business has been in Fairway for more than 50 years making some of the area's best birthday cakes from scratch. You can also pick up all the party supplies you need, like hats, cakes, napkins and whatever else you may need.

SPECIAL SHOPS

The Learning Tree, 4004 W. 83rd St., Prairie Village, KS 66208, 913-385-1234, www.toysandgifts.com**.** Located in the Corinth Square Shopping Center, this is not your typical toy store. You'll find lots of stuff to stimulate a child's curiosity and creativity. Check the website for activities, including artist and author visits, story and play times. Much of this happens in the downstairs Rainbow Room, which is a great place for birthday parties.

SHAWNEE, MERRIAM AND MISSION

WELCOME

Northeast Johnson County Area Chamber of Commerce, 5800 Foxridge Dr., # 100, Mission, KS 66202, 913-262-2141, www.nejcchamber.com**.**

Shawnee Area Chamber of Commerce, 15100 W. 67th St., # 202, Shawnee, KS 66217, 913-631-6545, www.cityofshawnee.org**.**

ASSISTANCE

Mommy and Me, 913-631-5200. Coordinated by the Shawnee Parks and Recreation Department at the Shawnee Civic Centre, this 90-minute program each week brings a parent and preschooler together with others their age for a song, story and snack. **Ages: 2 – 3.**

COMMUNITY CENTERS

Merriam Community Center, 5701 Merriam Dr., Merriam, KS 66203, 913-322-5550, www.merriam.org/parks**.** A number of youth and adult programs are offered here, along with a health club, basketball court and game room. There are meeting rooms available for parties and club events.

Shawnee Civic Centre, 13817 Johnson Dr., Shawnee, KS 66216, 913-631-5200. Throughout the day, the Civic Centre is filled with classes that teach children various skills, crafts and sports for those of all ages. These change seasonally, so visit the city website at www.cityofshawnee.org**.**

SPECIAL AREA PARKS AND PLAYGROUNDS

Antioch Park, 6501 Antioch Rd., Merriam. This 44-acre park is one of the most popular community parks in the metropolitan area. Facilities include an accessible play area for children, four picnic shelters and two small fishing lakes. Kids will also enjoy Old Dodge Town Play Town, complete with a general store and hotel.

Listowel Park, 71st and Quivira, Shawnee. This nine-acre park has a great playground shaped like a pirate ship, as well as a roller hockey field, walking trail and picnic tables.

Shawnee Mission Park, 7900 Renner Rd., Lenexa and Shawnee. This is the largest park in Johnson County and the most-visited park in the state of Kansas. It's got everything, including a 150-acre lake popular for boating, fishing and sailboarding; 12 shelters; numerous picnic areas; horseback and nature trails; playgrounds, an archery range; a swimming beach with bathhouse concessions; and marina. Shawnee Mission Park is home to Theatre in the Park, renowned for its outdoor productions each summer.

Shawnee Mission Park Marina/Heritage Park Marina – 913-888-1990. These marinas offer canoes, pedal boats, sail boats and fishing boats for rent in season.

Thomas A. Soetaert Aquatic Center, 13805 Johnson Drive, Shawnee, KS 66216, 913-631-0054. The features for this seasonal pool include a zero-depth toddler area with playground, tube and body slides, spray features, a lazy river, shade umbrellas, an instructional pool for swim programs, the bathhouse and the concession area. Ages: All. Fee.

West Flanders Park, 55th and Nieman Rd., Shawnee, 913-631-5200. This nine-acre park is home to a magical castle-themed playground, beautiful trees, and peaceful surroundings of the rose garden.

THINGS TO DO

Ice Sports, 19900 Johnson Dr., Shawnee, KS 66218, 913-441-3033, www.icesportskc.com**.** This facility is another great one for birthday parties and large family gatherings because of the indoor ice rink and the on-ice supervision provided if mom and dad can't skate. Bring the kids here to watch the Kansas City Outlaws Hockey Team practice. Lessons and public skating time are available. **Ages: 2 and up. Fee.**

Johnson County Museum of History, 6305 Lackman Rd., Shawnee, KS 66217, 913-631-6709, www.jocomuseum.org**.** The hands-on activities here and the rotating exhibits entertain kids and adults with information about the changes in Johnson County from the 1820s to today. Don't miss the 1950s All-Electric House. **Ages: All. Fee.**

Mission Bowl, 5399 Martway, Mission, KS 66201, 913-432-7000, www.missionbowl.com**.** A family-owned business since 1958, Mission Bowl was one of the first places in the city to offer regular cosmic bowling sessions with the flashing lights and fun music that kids love. During birthday parties, there's no smoking. Ask about kids' leagues and check their website for the names of kids who've bowled some great games. **Ages: All. Fee.**

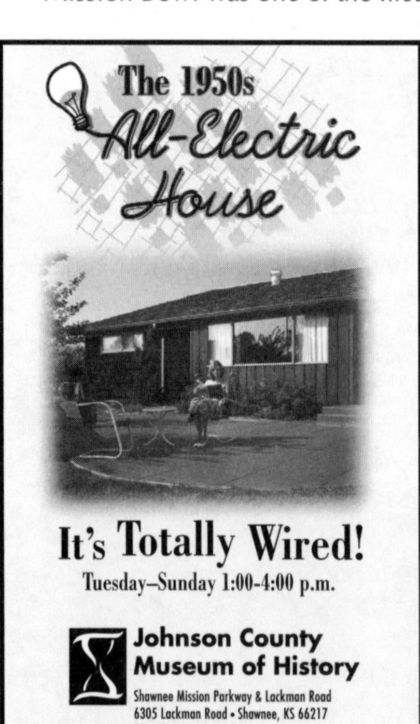

Old Shawnee Town, 11501 W. 57th St., Shawnee, KS 66216, 913-248-2360. More than 20 historic buildings and replicas dot the grounds of the Old West town, including the original 1843 Shawnee Jail, an undertakers shop and a smokehouse. This is the location of special events throughout the year, including a holiday tree lighting. **Ages: All. Fee.**

PowerPlay Family Entertainment Center, 13110 West 62nd Terrace Shawnee, KS 66216, 913-268-7200, www.powerplaykc.com. Send the kids up on the Rascal Rocket, let them wham about in a game of Whirley Ball, or go wild in LaserMania. This 80,000 square foot center also has educational things, such as painting ceramics and stuffing teddy bears. There's a separate play place for toddlers so they don't get run over by the big kids on their way to the indoor go-cart track or the monster-size tilt-a-whirl. It's a great place for birthday parties or family gathers. **Ages: All. Fee.**

Prairie Point Quilt Shop, 7341 Quivira Rd., Shawnee, KS 66216, 913-268-3333, www.prairiepoint.com. This popular fabric store offers summer and weekend workshops for kids teaching them quilting, embroidery and machine sewing. **Ages: 8 and up. Fee.**

Walls of Clay, 6015 Johnson Dr., Mission, KS 66202, 913-438-7623 or 16625 S. Midland, Shawnee, KS 66217, 913-438-7623. If your kids like to paint and create, bring them here to express themselves on pre-fired pottery or let them paint their handprints on ornaments or other gift items. It's something you can do together or let them create on their own. **Ages: All. Fee.**

Wonderscope Children's Museum, 5705 Flint, Shawnee, KS 66216, 913-268-4176, www.wonderscope.org. This former elementary school is now an interactive exploration center where kids can create and enjoy science, art, music and technology. Summer gardening and special events keep this award-winning center active all year. **Ages: 2 – 10. Fee.**

SPECIAL SHOPS

Doll Cradle Hospital, 5725 Nieman Rd., Shawnee, KS 66203, 913-631-1900, www.dollcradle.com. Rare and collectible dolls line the shelves, but kids really like the hospital that repairs dolls who've been loved a little too much.

Fun Party Services, 12119 Johnson Dr., Shawnee, KS 66216, 913-631-3717, www.funparty.cceasy.com. This place sells fun stuff for all ages, such as balloons, prizes, masks, costumes, toys, party supplies, wigs and more.

Pagah's, 11005 Johnson Dr., Shawnee, KS 66203, 913-962-6700. This family-owned restaurant treats you like family and cooks everything from scratch. Breakfast is served all day and the kids get excited about chocolate pancakes on the menu.

Velvet Créme Popcorn, 4710 Belinder Rd., Shawnee Mission, KS 66205, 913-236-7742, **www.velvetcremepopcorn.com.** Since 1937, this local company has made world-famous popcorn and wonderful candies, including homemade fudge, divinity and peanut brittle.

LENEXA, OLATHE, SPRING HILL

WELCOME

Lenexa Chamber of Commerce, 11180 Lackman Rd., Lenexa, KS 66219, 913-888-1414, www.lenexa.org.

Olathe Convention and Visitors Bureau, 142 N. Cherry, Olathe, KS 66061, 913-764-1050, www.olathe.org.

ASSISTANCE

Kaw Valley Center, 21350 W. 153rd St., Olathe, KS 66061, 913-322-4900, www.kawvalley.org. This non-profit organization provides a number of mental health and family counseling services for families with children up to 21 years old.

Moms Club of Olathe East, 913-768-7895. This unit of the national non-profit organization for stay-at-home moms meets at the New Hope Church on Black Bob Road.

THE GREAT OUTDOORS

Lenexa Parks and Recreation, 13420 Oak St., Lenexa, KS 66215, 913-541-8592, www.ci.lenexa,ks.us.

Olathe Parks and Recreation, 200 W. Santa Fe, Olathe, KS 66061, 913-971-6263, www.olatheks.org/activelife.

SPECIAL AREA PARKS AND PLAYGROUNDS

Black Bob Park, 145th and 151st St., Olathe. This park has everything you need – picnic shelters, a modern playground with tot swings, basketball, baseball, softball, soccer, fishing, swimming, a bike/pedestrian trail and a fitness course.

WHO WAS BLACK BOB?

THERE ARE LOTS OF FUN STORIES OUT THERE ABOUT WHO BLACK BOB WAS, BUT THE HISTORICAL SOCIETY TELLS US THAT BLACK BOB WAS THE NAME OF A SMALL TRIBE OF INDIANS HERE AND BLACK BOB WAS ALSO THE NAME GIVEN TO THEIR CHIEF.

Ernie Miller Park, 909 N. Hwy. 7, Olathe. The 114-acre park has been preserved in much of its natural state and features an outdoor amphitheatre, picnic shelters and three miles of nature trails. A part of the nature trail is handicap accessible.

Heritage Park, 16050 Pflumm Rd., Olathe. This is a massive park that includes a 45-acre lake, marina with pedal boats and sailboat rentals, lots of picnic areas and shelters, playgrounds, a golf course and driving range.

Prairie Center, 26325 W. 135th St., Olathe, KS 66061, 913-856-7669, www.kdwp.state.ks.us. Once all of this region was covered in the natural tallgrass prairie preserved on this 300 acres that includes six nature trails, a fishing pond and creeks. Programming for scout, school and churches groups is available upon request.

Sar-Ko-Par Trails Park, 87th St. and Lackman Rd., Lenexa. Lenexa's premier park has a swimming pool, skate park and walking trails, among other amenities. It is probably most recognizable for its huge art sculptures. There's a huge iron serpent for the kids to play on and then five floating bicycles out in the middle of the pond that make for fun conversations with kids.

Two Trails Park, 1000 N. Ridgeview, Olathe. This 18-acre park is home to Olathe's only skate park, as well as tennis courts and a huge shelter house.

THE CITY OF LENEXA IS NAMED AFTER THE WIFE OF SHAWNEE CHIEF THOMAS BLACKHOOF'S, WHO WAS VARIOUSLY RECORDED ON CENSUS RECORDS AS NA-NEX-SE AND LEN-AG-SEE. THE CHIEF AND HIS WIFE HAD BEEN EDUCATED IN OHIO BEFORE THEY TRAVELED TO THE SHAWNEE LANDS IN PRESENT-DAY JOHNSON COUNTY. SHE IS REPORTED TO HAVE BEEN A RESPECTED CHRISTIAN WOMAN.

The Spinach Capital of the U.S.

Maybe it will help get your kids to eat spinach if they know that Lenexa was once known as the Spinach Capital of the U.S. German, Swiss and Belgian immigrants purchased lands from the Shawnee and grew bumper crops in the fertile soil. In the 1930's, Lenexa became famous for its superior quality spinach. Popeye would have loved it!

THINGS TO DO

Ensor Farmsite and Museum, 18995 183rd St., Olathe, KS 66062, 913-592-4141. Built in 1909 by the Marshall Ensor Family, this former dairy farm now houses an outstanding display of early radio equipment, including a complete ham station licensed in 1922, which kids can operate. There are nine buildings on the farm, some dating to 1875. Visits are by appointment only. **Ages: 8 and up. Free.**

Family Adventure Laser Storm, 138 S. Clairborne, Olathe, KS 66062, 913-393-4386. This is an indoor laser tag arena with barriers and objects for players to hide behind. It's black-lit to add to the challenge of hitting your opponent with laser light. There's also an arcade and private birthday party room. **Ages: 5 and up. Fee.**

Frontier Pool, 15909 W. 127th St., Olathe, KS 66062, 913-971-6255. Fun slides and a huge sun deck are a part of this city-owned pool that has a family locker room. **Ages: All. Fee.**

Glow-Owl Cosmic Mini-Golf, Great Mall of the Great Plains, ext 217 off of I-35, Olathe, KS 66061, 913-764-5565. Mini golf moves to a higher plain on these indoor, glow-in-the-dark courses. **Ages: 2 and up. Fee.**

Gymboree, 12805 S. Mur-Len, Olathe, KS 66062, 913-469-1118, www.gymboree.com. A full line-up of classes that include music and playtime are designed to meet the growing skills and interests of kids. New challenges and experiences take place each week. **Ages: Birth to 6. Fee.**

Jeepers, The Great Mall of the Great Plains, exit 217 from I-35, Olathe, KS 66061, 913-393-3535, www.jeepers.com**.** This indoor amusement park features five rides, such as tilt-a-whirl and bumper cars. There's also a play pit and 75 arcade games, such as skee-ball and hoops. It's an extremely popular place for birthday parties. Check the website for coupons. **Ages: 2-12. Fee.**

Kansas Sports Center, 18145 W. 87th St. Pkwy., Lenexa, KS 66219, 913-888-4894, www.kansassportscenter.com**.** This center has a fully-lighted driving range, two 18-hole miniature golf courses, ten batting cages, and an outdoor pavilion for birthday parties. **Ages: All. Fee.**

Kidspark, 15296 W. 119th St., Olathe, KS 66062, 913-390-1411, www.kidspark.com**.** This hourly drop in child care program is open weekends and evenings and is great for birthday parties, summer camps, or just a few minutes of quiet time for mom. **Ages: 2 1/2 – 12. Fee.**

Legler Barn Museum, 14907 W. 87th St. Pkwy., Lenexa, KS 66215-4135, 913-492-0038. It is believed that Jesse James used this limestone barn on the Santa Fe Trail as a hideout during his escapades in the early 1860s. Today, kids enjoy the prairie schooner, the 1912 Lenexa railroad depot and caboose. There's also a sod hut and a children's play area that has antique toys. **Ages: 7 and up. Free.**

Mac and Seitz Baseball, 8875 Rosehill Rd., Lenexa KS 66215, 913-888-6961, www.macnseitz.com**.** Owned by Royals legends Mike McFarland and Kevin Seitzer, this huge facility has a number of indoor batting cages. Coaching is available for hitting, pitching, fielding and catching.
Ages: 5 and up. Fee.

Mahaffie Farmstead and Stagecoach Stop, 1100 N. Kansas City Rd., Olathe, KS 66061, 913-971-5111, www.olatheks.org/Visitors/Mahaffie/. Let your kids experience a stagecoach ride as the travelers of the 1860s did at this former stagecoach stop on the Santa Fe Trail that now operates as a living history museum. The Farmstead offers two weeks of historic day camps each summer. Across the street is Stagecoach Park with nature trails and a fishing pond. **Ages: All. Fee.**

Mill Creek Pool, 320 E. Poplar, Olathe, 66062, 913-971-6603. This pool is known for it's high dive area and the baby pool with play features. There are no slides at this pool. **Ages: All. Fee.**

New Century Airport, Olathe, 913-782-9216. A tour of the tower teaches children how air traffic and ground is controlled around the airport. Reservations required, limited number of people at a time. **Ages: 8th grade and up. Free.**

Olathe Community Theatre Assoc., 500 E. Loula, Olathe, KS 66051, 913-782-2990, www.olathetheatre.org. The company performs shows appropriate for family audiences ranging from drama and comedy to musicals. Each June, the theatre hosts a summer camp for children interested in acting. **Ages: 8-12. Fee.**

***Olathe Daily News*, 514 S. Kansas Ave., Olathe, KS 66061, 913-764-2211, ext. 153,** www.olathedailynews.com. Tours include a visit with a reporter or editor, and a look at various departments, computers, the press room and other tools used to put the newspaper on the street. **Ages: 1st grade and up. Free.**

Olathe Fire Department, 1225 S. Hamilton Circle, Olathe, KS 66061, 913-971-6333. The fire department welcomes families to drop by any of its six stations any time, but large groups require advance notice of about two weeks. Children can sit in fire trucks and practice the stop, drop and roll fire safety technique. **Ages: preschool and up. Free.**

Olathe Police Department, 501 E. 56 Highway, Olathe, KS 66061, 913-971-6610. Children are allowed to sit in a police car, visit the jail, the squad room and communications department on this 50 minute tour held on Monday evenings by appointment only. Advance reservations are required. **Ages: kindergarten and up. Free.**

Oregon Trail Pool, 1800 W. Dennis, Olathe, KS 66062, 913-971-6255. One of the busiest pools in the city because of its proximity to Oregon Trail Middle School, this one has lots of fun slides, but no diving facility. **Ages: All. Fee.**

Sadlers Indoor Racing, 325 N. Mur-Len Rd., Olathe, KS 66062, 913-768-7700, www.sadlersindoorracing.com**.** This is just too much fun for kids who dream of being NASCAR drivers! The 87,000 square feet of racing room includes two sizes of mini-cars that travel up to 50 miles per hour. The professional race staff will organize a race for the size and interest of your group. There's also a video arcade and a remote control car racing track. With a huge snack bar, this is a great place for birthday parties. Kids must be at least four feet, six inches to drive a car by themselves, but two seaters are available for little ones. **Ages: 8 and up. Fee.**

Smiley's Golf, 10195 Monticello Terr., Lenexa, KS 66227, 913-782-1323, www.smileysgolf.com**.** One of the two miniature golf courses here is haunted by ghosts, goblins and other fun creatures. The other is built like famous golf courses around the world. There's a game room, driving range and 18-hole executive course as well. **Ages: pre-school and up. Fee.**

Whittaker Flower Farm, 15855 W. 183rd St., Olathe, KS 66062, 913-592-3229, www.whittakerflowerfarm.com**.** Enjoy an educational stroll through six acres covered with more than 150 varieties of flowers, including a children's garden and English cottage. Open May through October. **Ages: All. Fee.**

FUN FOOD AND TREATS

Kansas Machine Shed, 12080 Strang Line Rd., Olathe, KS 66061, 913-780-2697. Life-sized tractors outside and toy tractors inside give kids lots to do while eating great country cooking and learning a bit about the agriculture industry of Kansas.

YOU SAY TOMATO—
IF YOU'RE NOT FROM KANSAS CITY, YOU MAY BE GUILTY OF MISPRONOUNCING OLATHE. O-LAY-THA IS A SHAWNEE INDIAN WORD THAT MEANS BEAUTIFUL, FOR WHEN THE AMERICAN INDIANS ROAMED THE LAND THAT IS NOW COVERED BY CONCRETE, SHOPPING MALLS AND OTHER MODERN INFLUENCES, THE LAND INSTEAD WAS COVERED WITH VERBENA AND OTHER BEAUTIFUL WILDFLOWERS. THE LAND WAS TRULY O-LAY-THA.

GARDNER AND EDGERTON

WELCOME

Gardner Area Chamber of Commerce, 900 E. Main St., Gardner, KS 66030, 913-856-6464, www.gardnerchamber.com.

THE GREAT OUTDOORS

Gardner Parks and Recreation, 120 E. Main, Gardner, KS 66030, 913-856-0936, www.gardnerkansas.com. Seasonal activities through the year include cheerleading, team sports, baby-sitting clinics, fire safety classes and various craft programs.

SPECIAL AREA PARKS AND PLAYGROUNDS

Cornerstone Park, 126 E. Washington, Gardner, KS 66030. The highlight of this four-acre park is the city pool, where swim lessons are offered. Basketball courts, tennis courts and a shelter round out the facilities here, where the city's Christmas in the Park celebration is held each December.

Veteran's Park, Center and Pawnee Sts., Gardner, KS 66030. This 41/2-acre park is home to two playgrounds with tot swings, a one-mile asphalt walking path and public restrooms. The focal point is the statue honoring Gardner veterans who have served in the U.S. military.

THINGS TO DO

Gardner Historical Museum, 204 W. Main St., Gardner, KS 66030, 913-856-4447, www.gardnerhistory.org. Each room in the historic home is filled with exhibits that highlight Gardner's early heritage along the Santa Fe Trail. Kids will enjoy the antique toys and one-room school house exhibit. Visit during January for special events on the history of Kansas statehood.

KC Pumpkin Patch, 29755 W. 191st St., Gardner, KS 66030, 913-484-6251, www.kcpumpkinpatch.com. Shoot a pumpkin from a cannon or throw one from a barn loft. Build a scarecrow, get lost in a straw maze, take a hay-ride, ride a train, and pick out your autumn pumpkin while here. Discounts offered to military families. **Ages: All. Fee.**

Lanesfield School Historic Site, 18745 S. Dillie Rd., Edgerton, KS 66021, 913-893-6645. The oldest one-room schoolhouse in the area was built in 1869 and was a mail stop along the Old Santa Fe Trail. It's now restored as a living history classroom with several special events through the year. While visiting, take a hike through the 78 acres of restored prairie. Picnic shelters are available. **Ages: All. Fee.**

STILWELL AND LOUISBURG (MIAMI COUNTY)

WELCOME

Louisburg Chamber of Commerce, 5 S. Peoria, Louisburg, KS 66053, 913-837-2826, www.louisburgks.net.

THINGS TO DO

Cedar Cove Feline Conservation Park, 3783 K-68 Highway, Louisburg, KS 66053, 913-837-5515, www.saveoursiberians.com. On 11 acres in Miami County, you'll find a center dedicated to the care of two Siberian tigers, five Bengal tigers, four cougars, two leopards, two bobcats and a rare South African caracal. The park has a picnic area and camping facilities and offers tours and meeting space by appointment only. **Ages: All. Fee.**

Heartland Therapeutic Riding School, 19655 Antioch Rd., Stilwell, KS 66085, 913-897-3939. Since 1978, Heartland's professional instructors have worked with the needs of emotionally, mentally and physically disabled children, teaching them how to ride. **Ages: 2 and up. Fee.**

Kirin Farms Riding School, 18230 Metcalf, Stilwell, KS 66085, 913-533-2450. For more than 25 years, Sandy Longan has been teaching area children to ride Hunt Seat or English. The farm is open year-round and provides everything but the boots for those of any skill level who want to learn to ride. **Ages: 6 and up. Fee.**

Louisburg Cider Mill, P.O. 670, Louisburg, KS 66053, 913-837-5202, www.cidermill.com. Take U.S. 69 south to K-68 for cold cider, fresh apples and hot donuts any time throughout the year. Apples are pressed into cider every day from September through November and you can watch as they make cider donuts. It's a great place to get your autumn pumpkins and gourds. The cider mill is home to Lost Trail Root Beer, an eastern Kansas family recipe. **Ages: All. Fee for purchases.**

Powell Observatory, 913-837-5305, www.askconline.org**.** Just off 263rd and U.S. 69 in Lewis-Young Park northwest of Louisburg, this observatory has a 30-inch computer controlled telescope that is open to the public for viewing the night skies November through April. The site is also home to a Junior Astronomers program and is available for parties and special events. You have to be at least 36 inches tall to peer through the telescope. **Ages: 10 and up. Fee.**

FARTHER OUT—IN FRANKLIN COUNTY

Drop Zone Paintball Park, near Baldwin City, 785-841-1884, www.dropzonepaintball.com**.** This field about 30 minutes west of Kansas City has become one of the most popular paintball fields in the Midwest with three wooded fields and a huge castle field. For the really aggressive player, there are two air ball fields. Drop Zone has retail outlets in Olathe and Gladstone. **Ages: 10 and up. Fee.**

WEEKEND GETAWAYS

TOPEKA, KS

A field trip or weekend getaway to the state capitol is more than just a civics lesson, but an opportunity to explore history and nature, and take a spin on an antique carousel.

One of the nation's newest national historic sites opened to the public in May 2004 in the former Monroe School on the city's southeast side. The Monroe School was one of four African-American schools in Topeka in 1954 when the landmark Supreme Court case
Brown vs. Topeka Board of Education ended desegregation in publicly funded schools. The building has been restored to its condition of the early 1950s and includes numerous interactive exhibits that encourage children to explore the concept of racial segregation.

The Kansas Museum of History tells the story of Kansas from its first inhabitants to modern-day culture. There is a children's discovery center where kids can explore hands-on a Cheyenne buffalo-hide tepee, an 1866 log house and a locomotive with dining and sleeping cars.

More history and lots of old-fashioned fun is found at the Ward-Meade Park, a six-acre living history town that includes a train depot, log cabin, one-room school house and a drug-store where old-fashioned sodas are still served. Ward-Meade Park is often the site of special events that bring the early days of Topeka to life for children of the 21st Century.

A visit to Topeka with the kids must include Gage Park, which includes a 1908 carousel that is still in working condition. Gage Park is also home to Black Bear Woods, where you can watch black bears in their native habitat, and the Topeka Zoo, famous for its Gorilla Encounter and the Tropical Rain Forest. Of course, there's a children's zoo where kids can pet and feed farm animals.

The Combat Air Museum is another good stop if the kids are interested in military or aviation history. This is the only museum in the world to display operational aircraft from every arm conflict utilizing powered aircraft.

Each September, Topeka celebrates its American Indian heritage with the Shawnee County Allied Tribes All Nations

Powwow. Call 800-235-1030 or visit www.topekacvb.org. For more details on a visit to Topeka or other Kansas weekend getaways, pick up a copy of Shifra Stein's *Day Trips® from Kansas City*, available at area bookstores and on-line at www.kckidsguide.com.

JEFFERSON CITY, MO

Fourth grade is the ideal time for Missouri school children to visit the state capitol as a part of their unit of study on state history. Anyone, school-aged or not, interested in the Lewis and Clark Expedition will enjoy a trip to the city named for Thomas Jefferson, who authorized the infamous journey to the Pacific. The newest addition to the impressive Missouri State Park System is just east of Jefferson City and is named for co-captain of the expedition. Clark's Hill/Norton State Historic Site, at the mouth of the Osage River, also includes American Indian archeology in the visitors' center that details William Clark's observations here in June 1806.

The oldest buildings in Jeff City, located at Jefferson Landing State Historic Site, bring to life the time where steamboats stopped at this western outpost in the 1830s and later, when train travel was the primary method of reaching the state capitol. The Amtrak station is located at Jefferson Landing. Consider taking Amtrak from Kansas City or Lee's Summit, walk around the capitol grounds and return the same day, if you like.

Another route to Jefferson City is via the Katy Trail, the wonderful hiking/biking trail that crosses 225 miles of the state along former railroad tracks that mostly follows the Missouri River. Jefferson City is one of several accesses to the trail, so you may wish to bring bikes with you to ride this area of the trail.

Take the kids to the capitol building on Tuesday, Wednesday or Thursday mornings to watch the legislature when in session January through May. On the first floor is the Missouri Museum, which includes more on Lewis and Clark and others of influence in the Show-Me State's history. The state capitol is often known as the home of the Thomas Hart Benton Mural on the third floor. Painted in 1936, the mural covers all four walls of the House Lounge and reflects the legends, history, lore and industry of Missouri. It is considered one of the Missouri artist's most ingenious and valuable works. Tours of the capitol, given daily on

the hour from 8 a.m. until 4 p.m. include the Benton Mural.

Kids will have a great time at the Runge Nature Center, a Missouri Department of Conservation showpiece that details the rivers and wetlands, farmland and caves that make up Missouri. Hiking trails, outdoor demonstration and naturalist-guided programs are offered over the 112 acres seven days a week.

One last stop in Jeff city that everyone in the family will love is at the Central Dairy at 610 Madison. Here you'll find the most fabulous ice cream sundaes made out of any of about 40 flavors of ice cream made right on the premises. Bring a cooler to take some home. Central Dairy still delivers milk door-to-door in Jefferson City, just like the good ole days.

For more information on visiting Jefferson City, go to www.visitjeffersoncity.com or call 800-769-4183. For more details on Jefferson City or other Missouri weekend getaways, pick up a copy of Shifra Stein's *Day Trips® from Kansas City*, available at area bookstores and on-line at www.kckidsguide.com.

LAKE OF THE OZARKS

Located 165 miles southeast of Kansas City, the Lake of the Ozarks is considered the Midwest's premiere playground for kids and grown-ups alike. The lake covers 59,600 acres with more shoreline than the state of California and is surrounded by 100 marinas, dozens of waterfront restaurants, and hundreds of shops, services and businesses. Almost every water sport known to man is available here, as well a fabulous golfing, camping, fishing, horseback riding and more. You name it. If it's fun, it's available somewhere in the communities of the Lake of the Ozarks.

The Lake was created in the 1930s with the construction of Bagnell Dam, a massive structure that generates electrical power for much of the Midwest and is the focal point of the Lake. The dam is no longer open for tour, but you'll find a great museum on its construction and life in central Missouri before and after, at the Willmore Lodge, northeast of the dam on Business 54. Once the administrative center for Union Electric, the building serves as a visitors center for the Lake area and a museum. There's a scale model of the dam, audio/video interviews with workers who helped build the dam, lots of historical photos and much more.

A unique geographical feature to the Lake area is the more

than 300 caves in the three county area, three of them open to the public. Bridal Cave is the oldest in the area and one of the most scenic in the country. It is the site of a legendary Indian wedding ceremony and is accessible by car or boat. Jacob's Cave is the largest in the area and the only walk-through cave that is wheelchair accessible. It features the world's largest geode and prehistoric mastodon bones. Tours of Ozark Caverns are given by handheld lanterns and highlight fabulous waterfalls and rock formations.

Although not as well known as Branson, the Lake of the Ozarks has its share of family-oriented music shows. Among them is the Main Street Music Hall, in The Landing on Main Street, on Hwy. 54 in Osage Beach. The show includes new and old country music, rock 'n' roll and gospel, with patriotic tunes and hits from the '40s, '50s and '60s.

There are, without a doubt, hundreds of accommodations to choose from in the Lake area, but new on the scene and a must with the kids is the Timber Falls Indoor Waterpark at Tan-Tar-A. The 20,000 square foot park centers on a three-story treehouse topped with a giant tipping bucket that cascades up to 700 gallons of water every few minutes. The park also features four water slides, activity pool, oversized whirlpool and lazy river for tube floating.

The *Lake of the Ozarks Vacation and Service Guide* provides a comprehensive list of the numerous resorts, hotels, condos and cottages available for rent, as well as restaurants and family-friendly attractions. It is available through the Lake of the Ozarks Convention and Visitors Bureau by calling 800-386-5253 or visiting www.funlake.com.

Read more about the seasonal activities and attractions at the Lake in Shifra Stein's *Day Trips® from Kansas City*, available in area bookstores or on-line at www.kckidsguide.com.

OMAHA, NE

Just a quick jaunt up I-29 from Kansas City is one of the best family weekend destinations you'll find anywhere. Long renowned as one of the world's best, the Henry Doorly Zoo includes a fabulous aquarium, an indoor jungle, a domed desert and an exhibit where humans, not apes, are on display.

Imagine playing tug-of-war with a 400-pound gorilla or patty-

cake with his 200-pound mate. It's possible in the Hubbard Gorilla Valley. The three-acre exhibit is designed so that gorillas have a full view of human spectators through floor to ceiling plexi-glass windows.

The gorillas may crawl on top of tunnels that visitors must pass through and peer down at them from above. Another tunnel allows children to crawl in the midst of the gorillas and pop up in one of two five-feet tall plexi-glass bubbles.

The most popular activity for gorillas and humans is tug-of-war. A six-foot length of rope passes through a secure-window where a gorilla or two is always anxious to give you and a couple of friends a test of strength and stamina.

If you fail at that, try a simple game of patty-cake. Line your paws up with the massive hands of the gorilla and see who has the quickest and most adept reactions. Another interactive area places a steering wheel on both sides of the glass window and you and your favorite gorilla can see who is the better driver.

There's much more entertainment at the Kingdoms of the Seas Aquarium where you are surrounded by sharks, sting-rays and other less-threatening aquatic life, such as puffins and puffer fish. But the show-stealing entertainment is penguins, seen through a 60-foot long, 25-foot high window extending both above and five feet below water level. They frolic and dive underwater while remaining stately and austere in their tuxedos above water.

The Henry Doorly Zoo is also known for its Desert Dome, which features desert life from around the world in the planet's largest geodesic dome. Underneath is Kingdoms of the Night, the world's largest nocturnal exhibit, which is run on a reverse-light sequence that allows daytime visitors to see nocturnal creatures when they are most active.

Changing every time you visit is the Lied Jungle, a living jungle covering more than 1 1/2 acres under eight stories of sky-lit glass. The paved walkway allows you to roam eye-to-eye with leopards, tapirs and hornbills while examining the plants and trees that make up the rainforests of Asia, Africa and South America.

Not all in Omaha is about the zoo. The city has a great children's museum where you can spend the night while earning various scouting badges, and a Science Center with lots of hands-on activities. The Mormon Trail passes through Omaha, so there are a number of sites and attractions related to that historic element of our nation's development. Check out the city's website at www.visitomaha.com.

For more ideas on weekend getaways, pick up a copy of Shifra Stein's *Day Trips® from Kansas City*, available at area bookstores and on-line at www.kckidsguide.com.

DES MOINES, IA

Just about three hours north of Kansas City along I-35 is Des Moines, Iowa and lots of fun things to do with the family. The city is home to the Science Center of Iowa, a new addition to downtown on Market, between Third and Sixth Streets. Six experience platforms features themes such as: "Science Is Where You Find It," "Who Are We?," "What On Earth?," "When Things Get Moving," "Why The Sky?," and "Small Discoveries." It's a great place to let the imagination go wild!

If your kids can't imagine what it was like to grow up on a farm, in Iowa or elsewhere, plan a day at the Living History Farms. This 600-acre open-air museum features five time periods spanning 300 years. Each day visitors can participate in real life activities such as soap making or harvesting during each time period. Visit an Ioway Indian Village, an 1850s pioneer farm, a post Civil War community, a 1900 horse-powered farm or a more modern agriculture center.

After such an educational experience, reward the kids with a visit to Adventureland Park, with more than 100 rides, shows and attractions. Adventureland has a water park, a crazy ride called "The Sidewinder," and a hotel adjacent to the property.

Des Moines is home to the Blank Park Zoo, the baby giraffes and the big cats exhibit. Stop by a favorite with the kids, the petting zoo, and the new flamingo area. Indoors, enjoy more than 20 exhibits on the cycle of water that begins in an inhabited researcher's cabin high in the mountains on a warm winter day. Along the trail falling snow and dripping icicles form a stream. Through the foliage visitors will see a pair of lynx that have made their den. The Subterranean Biome contains many fascinating exhibits including the Coral Reef, an incredible visual treat for all ages. Here, visitors view vivid fish and other sea creatures moving through their colorful coral reef home.

A great time to visit Des Moines may be in August for the infamous Iowa State Fair, the nation's oldest and the inspiration behind the Rogers and Hammerstein musical State Fair.

For more information on a visit to Des Moines, go to www.seedesmoines.com or call 800-451-2625. For more ideas on weekend getaways, pick up a copy of Shifra Stein's *Day Trips® from Kansas City*, available at area bookstores and on-line at www.kckidsguide.com.

For more ideas of fun places to travel with your family, visit the website, **www.kckidsguide.com** and click the tab

"Other Fun Places."

From national parks to little known communities in our country to destinations around the globe, author Diana Lambdin Meyer has traveled there with her family, and takes you there as well with her experiences, photos, and contacts for you to set up a great vacation with your family!

ABOUT THE AUTHORS

DIANA LAMBDIN MEYER

Diana Lambdin Meyer and her husband, Bruce, live in Parkville with their son, Bradley, and fuzzy, white cat Snowbelle. Long before they were married, Bruce encouraged Diana to pursue a writing career independent of traditional employment, and that step came in 1995. She now writes for numerous newspapers and magazines around the country, including *The Kansas City Star*. Bruce's photos often accompany her work.

Diana is an award-winning member of the Midwest Travel Writers Association and the Society of American Travel Writers. She is a contributing editor for Fodor's Travel Publications, Globe-Pequot Press, and Travel America, The Crafts Report, The Quilter and various AAA publications. Her novel "Head Rites," a women's contemporary fiction work focusing on environmental issues, is available at www.kckidsguide.com or www.amazon.com.

Her journalism career has taken Diana around the world, but if home is where the heart is, Diana's is the southern Illinois grain farm where she was raised and that remains in the Lambdin family. The love of travel Diana and her family share have enriched their lives through an increased awareness of cultural diversity, an appreciation for history and the natural environment, and a curiosity for the oddities of life.

An accomplished speaker and workshop presenter, Diana welcomes invitations to share her books and experiences with your group. She may be contacted through www.kckidsguide.com.

ABOUT THE AUTHORS

SHIFRA STEIN

Writer, author, artist and workshop presenter, Shifra Stein's many guidebooks include the popular *Day Trips®* series for Globe-Pequot Press. She published the first edition of *A Kid's Guide to Kansas City* in the late 1980s. She is now the grandmother of Max and Erica. A native of Kansas City, she is also the author of *Wild About Kansas City Barbecue, Unlocking the Power Within; Journaling for Personal and Professional Growth*. These books are available for purchase at www.kckidsguide.com.

A skilled keynote speaker and workshop presenter, Ms. Stein offers both travel presentations and creativity training seminars. She is a firm believer in the deep connection between art and healing. Her dynamic Art For The Health Of It, Healing Power of Color, and Watercolor Workshops demonstrate the dynamic relationship between art and health. Her Journaling Workshops and Creativity Classes combine expressive writing and the visual arts together in motivational presentations that help promote well being, reduce stress, and encourage creativity. These workshops have been offered around the country through organizations, and arts and educational venues.

Ms. Stein is also an accomplished artist. Working in gouache, watercolor, mixed media, and Japanese masa paper, she has developed a unique style that has been featured in regional and national publications. For more information on her work or to schedule Ms. Stein for a speaking engagement, see her website www.shifrastein.com.

New Places to Visit in Kansas City

INDEX

178

Notes